Author

Walt Henrichsen committed his life to Christ while an engineering student at Central College, Pella, Iowa. He later attended Western Theological Seminary in Holland, Michigan.

Walt came in contact with The Navigators while working in the follow-up office of the San Francisco Billy Graham Crusade in 1958. After graduating from seminary, he was involved in a training program in Colorado Springs. He then joined a Navigator ministry in Los Angeles, and later went to Mexico for a Wycliffe Bible Translators jungle training camp.

He has ministered in Kalamazoo, Michigan; served as southwestern regional director; and was personnel director worldwide for The Navigators. Today Walt is Deputy Director of the Pacific Area Navigators. He, his wife, Leette, and three children live in Christchurch, New Zealand.

To his present responsibility Walt has brought a deep and practical knowledge of the Bible as well as experience and know-how in training men and women to grow in their faith and reach others for Christ.

Un'dər stand'

A straightforward approach to interpreting the Bible.

Walter A. Henrichsen

NAVPRESS

A MINISTRY OF THE NAVIGATORS

P.O. Box 1659
Colorado Springs
Colorado 80901

The Navigators is an international,
interdenominational Christian organization.
Jesus Christ gave His followers a Great
Commission in Matthew 28:19, "Go therefore
and make disciples of all nations . . . ."
The primary aim of the Navigators is to
help fulfill that commission by making
disciples and developing disciplemakers
in every nation.

Printed in the United States of America

Contents

Dedicated to
the glory of the resurrected Christ
to whom I owe my all

Foreword

A real need of this volcanic hour is a straightforward approach to biblical interpretation. We need solid food . . . not just mere crumbs. We need to learn the art of chewing . . . not just sucking on milk bottles. We need to think with some individual moral honesty . . . not continue the process of religious brainwashing. A Christian leader has said, "Christianity used to be a trumpet call to holy living, high thinking and solid Bible study; now it is a timid and apologetic invitation to a mild discussion."

Walt Henrichsen believes that the Holy Scriptures are a vital necessity and not just a speculative luxury. Hence, he pulls the plug in his book with the focus on results, not just activity in knowing God's Word.

The author is a man who sees it big, but has the capacity to keep it simple. As a theologian, pastor, Bible teacher, counselor and father, he has placed the "cookies" down on the lower shelf where all can learn to reach and eat.

Frank E. Gaebelein has stated the case well: "Christianity is peculiarly a religion of a single book. Take away the Bible and you have destroyed the means by which God chose to present through successive ages His revelation to man. It follows, then , that knowledge of the Bible is an indispensable prerequisite for growth in the Christian life."

Biblical interpretation is more than just an intellectual game that theologians play. It opens up our lives in Christ. It is the Christian life made full. This life is to be enjoyed as we learn the basic "ground rules" and then pass them on to others. Thanks to Walt Henrichsen for taking this subject out of the libraries of the seminaries and out of the vocabulary of the "specialist," and bringing it down to where each of us is living today.

ROBERT D. FOSTER
Lost Valley Ranch
June, 1976

1 Interpretation Is for Everyone

To Become more obedient to the heavenly vision. To go out & share —

This book has been written for those who enjoy studying the Bible and wonder if they are doing it correctly. You no doubt have heard it said, "Everyone has his own interpretation of the Bible," or, "The two things people can never agree on are religion and politics."

If such assertions are true, then Christianity is meaningless and the Bible has no message for us. If an individual can make the Bible say what he wants it to say, then the Bible cannot guide him. It is merely a weapon in his hands to support his own ideas. The Bible was not written with that purpose in mind.

Most books on the subject of biblical interpretation are quite lengthy and involved. Produced for those familiar with Hebrew, Aramaic and Greek, the languages in which Scripture was originally written, they seek to treat the subject in a thorough and scholarly way. For example, they contain detailed explanations of allegories, similes, metaphors, and other language uses. They explore trends in

11

theology, such as the impact of neoorthodoxy on the church, or the effect of liberalism in denying the supernatural.

This book presents basic biblical laws of interpretation in simple terms, and in so doing provides a functional tool for every Christian who wants to understand and apply Scripture.

Every person lives his life with certain basic assumptions. These assumptions vary from one situation to another. For example, if you were to fly to Japan, you would have to assume at least four things:

1. The pilot knows how to fly the aircraft.

2. The plane will arrive safely.

3. The immigration people in Japan will honor your passport.

4. You will be able to accomplish your intended purpose for going.

In our study of the laws or rules for interpreting the Bible we must also assume certain things:

1. The Bible is authoritative.

2. The Bible contains its own laws of interpretation, which, when properly understood and applied, will yield the correct meaning to a given passage.

3. The primary aim of interpretation is to discover the author's meaning.

4. Language can communicate spiritual truth.

These assumptions will appear frequently in the principles listed in this book. Some are rules as well as assumptions and will appear as such.

These assumptions make a significant difference in the whole approach to Bible study. To study, interpret and be able to apply the Bible *correctly* are the goals of every conscientious Christian. Before noting how these four assumptions and the subsequent principles affect the study of Scripture, it is worth noting that there are four basic steps in studying the Bible correctly. They are:

- **OBSERVATION**—answers the question, "What do I see?" Here the Bible student approaches the text as a detective. No detail is unimportant; no stone is left unturned. Every observation is carefully listed for further thought and comparisons.

- **INTERPRETATION**—answers the question, "What does it mean?" Here the interpreter bombards the text with questions such as, "What did these details mean to the people to whom they were given?" / "Why did he say this?" / "How will this work?" / "What is the major idea he is seeking to comunicate?"

- **CORRELATION**—answers the question, "How does this relate to the rest of what the Bible says?" The Bible student must do more than just examine individual passages. He must coordinate his study with what else the Bible says on the subject. An accurate understanding of the Bible on any subject takes into account *all* the Bible says about that subject.

- **APPLICATION**—answers the question, "What does it mean to me?" This is the goal of the other three steps. An expert in the field said it succinctly, "Observation and interpretation without application is abortion." The Bible is God speaking. His Word demands a response. That response needs to be nothing less than obedience to the revealed will of God.

These four steps to Bible study are guided by the ground rules of interpretation. The psalmist said, "With all my heart I have sought Thee; do not let me wander from Thy commandments. Thy Word I have treasured in my heart, that I may not sin against Thee" (Psalm 119:10, 11). His words echo the heart cry of the dedicated Christian, whose goal is to so saturate himself with God's Word that he begins to think and react in a Godlike way. To do this, the Bible student must so familiarize himself with these ground rules that they become part of his Scripture investigation.

The rules of interpretation are divided into four categories: General, Grammatical, Historical and Theological.

General Principles of Interpretation (chapter 2) are principles that deal with the overall subject of interpretation. They are universal in nature rather than being limited to special considerations, which are listed in the other three sections.

Grammatical Principles of Interpretation (chapter 3) are principles that deal with the text itself. They lay down the ground rules for understanding the words and sentences in the passage under study.

Historical Principles of Interpretation (chapter 4) are principles that deal with the background or context in which the books of the Bible were written. Political, economic and cultural situations are important in considering the historical aspect of your study of the Word of God.

Theological Principles of Interpretation (chapter 5) are principles that deal with the formation of Christian doctrine. They are, of necessity, "broad" rules, for doctrine must take into consideration all that the Bible says about a given subject. Though they tend to be somewhat complicated, they are nonetheless important, for they play a profound role in shaping that body of belief you call your convictions.

2 General Principles of Interpretation

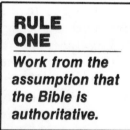

RULE ONE

Work from the assumption that the Bible is authoritative.

In matters of religion the Christian submits either consciously or unconsciously to one of the following as his ultimate authority: Tradition, Reason or the Scriptures. The official, historical position of the Roman Catholic Church has been to make tradition the final court of appeal. The doctrine of the virgin Mary is an example. What the Bible teaches about Mary is interpreted in accordance with how the Catholic Church has traditionally viewed her.

Rationalism has occupied center stage in much of Protestantism. Liberalism and Modernism are terms coined to describe this approach. For them, the conclusion that the mind draws is the final court of appeal. What the human mind cannot accept as reasonable is rejected. Likewise, reason is left to decide what is fundamental to a faith in God. For example, a person embracing this approach may conclude that belief in the virgin birth of Christ is neither rational nor essential, and the biblical teaching can therefore be denied.

The evangelical Christian looks to the Bible as his final court of appeal. Belief in Jesus' virgin birth is embraced because the Bible teaches it. What the church has historically believed concerning the virgin Mary must be interpreted by the Scriptures and not vice versa.

This is not to suggest that there is no validity in each of the three forms of authority. Adherents to each of the above systems of thought would readily agree to the importance of each of the others. In case of conflict, however, the question is, which vote counts? If tradition, reason and Scripture differ as to how to view Mary and the virgin birth of Christ, which authority is the final arbitrator? *The first law of interpretation says the Bible is the final court of appeal.*

The subject of biblical authority is often tied to the question of the inspiration of the Scriptures. A person cannot submit to the Bible as his authority if it is not the inspired Word of God. The same issue arose during the ministry of Jesus Christ on earth. He taught "as one having authority" (Matthew 7:29). But on what was His authority based? How can we know if He truly is the Christ as He claims to be?

In answer to these probing questions, Jesus said, "If any man is willing to do His [God's] will, he shall know of the teaching, whether it is of God, or whether I speak from Myself" (John 7:17). "If you will *do* what I ask you to do, then you will *know* if what I am saying is right or not," is what Jesus basically said. If you will *do,* then you will *know.* Doing comes before knowing. Commitment comes before knowledge. Hundreds of years ago St. Augustine put it this way, "I believe; therefore I know."

Authority has to do with the will, with obedience and with

doing. Inspiration concerns the intellect, understanding and knowledge. The question of inspiration must follow authority. Just as it is only after you do what Jesus asks you to do that you know that He is the Christ, so also only after you have submitted yourself to the authority of the Bible and obeyed it will you know that it is the inspired Word of God.

The demand that commitment come before knowledge is not unique to the Christian faith. It is common, everyday experience for all people. In the introduction we talked about the use of assumptions. We used the illustration of going to Japan. By making those assumptions you simply made a commitment before you knew what would happen. You didn't *know* the authorities would let you into Japan. You *assumed* they would, and *committed* yourself to that assumption before you *knew*.

Expanding the illustration, let us say you go to the pilot before takeoff and inquire about the safety of the huge aircraft.

"Will it really get me to Tokyo?" you ask.

"Certainly," the captain assures you.

You probe further. "But what about the airplane that went down in the Pacific a number of months ago. Can you *guarantee* that the plane will arrive in Japan safely?"

"No," says the captain, "I can't guarantee it. But climb aboard and when we arrive (if we arrive), you will know."

That is commitment before knowledge. You are willing to commit yourself and take the risk because it is a long swim to Japan.

Therefore in Bible study you begin with the issue of authority. It and the question of inspiration which naturally follows are answered when you submit to the Word of God. You may study inspiration as a separate topic, but you only *know* the Bible to be the inspired Word of God as you place yourself under its authority.

As you seek to submit yourself to what the Scriptures say, it is important to understand that authority in the Bible is expressed in various ways.

1. A person acts in an authoritative manner, and the passage explains whether the act is approved or disapproved. For example, in the Garden of Eden, "The serpent said to the woman, 'You surely shall not die' " (Genesis 3:4). We know this to be wrong because Adam and Eve in fact did die.

King David wanted to build a temple for God, so Nathan said to him, "Go, do all that is in your mind, for the Lord is with you" (II Samuel 7:3). Nathan in an authoritative way told David what to do, but we read that his advice was wrong and that God did *not* want David to build the temple (verses 4-17).

After the Jerusalem Council (Acts 15), the Apostle Peter visited the church in Antioch of Syria, and ate with the Gentiles. Paul says of Peter, "Prior to the coming of certain men from James, he used to eat with the Gentiles; but when they came, he began to withdraw and hold himself aloof, fearing the party of the circumcision [Jewish Christians]" (Galatians 2:12). We know that his act of separating from Gentile Christians was wrong, for Paul rebuked him for it and then explained why it was wrong.

2. A person acts in an authoritative manner and the passage does not indicate approval or disapproval. In this case the action must be judged on the basis of what the rest of the Bible teaches on the subject. For example, Abraham and Sarah go to Egypt because of a famine in Canaan (Genesis 12:10-20). Fearful that Pharaoh might kill him in order to take beautiful Sarah for himself, Abraham says to his wife, "Please say that you are my sister so that it may go well with me because of you, and that I may live on account of you" (12:13). Was this a cowardly thing for Abraham to do? The

passage does not say. You are left for your conclusion to your own understanding of what the rest of Scripture has to say on the subject.

You will have to decide in your mind whether Abraham was wrong in his actions or not, and this is precisely what interpreting the Bible is all about. This book will not seek to give you the "correct" interpretation, but will simply help you choose for yourself the correct basis for coming to your conclusions.

After Lot lost his wife when God destroyed Sodom and Gomorrah, he and his two daughters went to live in a cave in the mountains above Zoar. Fearful that they would never marry and thus die childless, the two daughters took matters into their own hands. On two successive nights they made their father drunk, and then they had sexual intercourse with him, one on each night. They became pregnant and bore sons, Moab and Ben-ammi, by their father (see Genesis 19:30-38).

Yet Peter says that Lot was a righteous man. "He [God] condemned the cities of Sodom and Gomorrah to destruction by reducing them to ashes, having made them an example to those who would live ungodly thereafter; and . . . He rescued righteous Lot, oppressed by the sensual conduct of unprincipled men" (II Peter 2:6, 7). Was what happened in the cave of Zoar a righteous act? The passage does not say. The Scriptures do, however, have a great deal to say about the kind of behavior that took place in the cave of Zoar, and the action can be judged on the basis of those many teachings.

3. God or one of His representatives states the mind and will of God. These are often in the form of commandments. For example, Jesus said, "A new commandment I give to you, that you love one another, even as I have loved you, that you also love one another. By this all men will know that

you are My disciples, if you have love for one another" (John 13:34, 35).

Some commands, however, are for immediate circumstances and are not meant to be universally applied. God said to Noah, "Make for yourself an ark of gopher wood; you shall make the ark with rooms, and shall cover it inside and out with pitch" (Genesis 6:14). Jesus said to two of His disciples, "Go into the village opposite you, and immediately you will find a donkey tied there and a colt with her; untie them, and bring them to Me" (Matthew 21:2). Because God told Noah to build an ark, it does not mean we must feel it is the will of God that we build arks; nor do we go around untying donkeys and bringing them to Jesus. The context and nature of the command indicates whether or not it is to be universally applied.

All Scripture is authoritative, but there are parts you are not to follow. You must be careful, however, not to use fancy logic to avoid doing what you know the will of God to be for you.

Secular man is drifting farther and farther from the biblical absolutes. This in turn puts pressure on the church to take a fresh approach to the biblical commands regarding such things as divorce and a wide variety of moral questions. More often than not this fresh approach is nothing more than the gross immorality that caused the fall of Sodom and Gomorrah. Such trends originate in an unwillingness to submit to the authority of the Bible.

For the Christian, the Bible is and will always remain authoritative.

RULE TWO

The Bible interprets itself; Scripture best explains Scripture.

The Bible tells us that one of the ... interpreters of God's Word was the devil.

"Now the serpent was more crafty than any beast of the field which the Lord God had made. And he said to the woman, 'Indeed, has God said, "You shall not eat from any tree of the garden"?' And the woman said to the serpent, 'From the fruit of the trees of the garden we may eat; but from the fruit of the tree which is in the middle of the garden, God has said, "You shall not eat from it or touch it, lest you die."' And the serpent said to the woman, 'You surely shall not die! For God knows that in the day you eat from it your eyes will be opened, and you will be like God, knowing good and evil'" (Genesis 3:1-5).

Earlier God had said, "From any tree of the garden you may eat freely; but from the tree of the knowledge of good and evil you shall not eat, for in the day that you eat from it you shall surely die" (Genesis 2:16, 17). Satan did not deny that God said those words. Rather he twisted them, giving them a meaning they did not have. Such error takes place by omission and addition.

Omission—quoting only that part which suits you while leaving out the rest. There are two types of death in the Bible, physical and spiritual. Physical death is the separation of the soul from the body. Spiritual death is the separation of the soul from God. When God told Adam, "You shall surely die" (Genesis 2:17), He was referring to both spiritual and physical death. When the serpent said to Eve, "You surely shall not die" (3:4), he was purposely omitting the fact of spiritual death.

Addition—saying more than the Bible says. In her conversation with Satan, Eve quotes what God told her husband. But she adds to His Word the phrase, "or touch it" (Genesis 3:3). You can twist Scripture by making it say more than it, in fact, says. Usually the motive is a desire to make God's command unreasonable and thus unworthy of being obeyed.

When you study the Bible, let it speak for itself. Neither add to it, nor subtract from it. Let the Bible be its own commentary. Compare Scripture with Scripture.

For example, Isaiah says, "Therefore the Lord Himself will give you a sign: Behold, a virgin will be with child and bear a son, and she will call His name Immanuel" (Isaiah 7:14). In Hebrew the word translated in many versions as "virgin" can actually be translated either "young woman" or "virgin." This same verse is quoted by Matthew in reference to the virgin birth of Jesus Christ (Matthew 1:23). In Greek, however, the word has only *one* meaning, "virgin." In other words, Matthew interprets the word for us and we translate Isaiah's expression as "virgin."

We will usually apply this rule to the great truths of the Bible rather than to specific verses. Such a truth is *assurance of salvation.* Individual verses can be quoted on both sides of the question of whether or not we can lose our salvation. Paul said to the Galatians, "You have fallen from grace" (Galatians 5:4). Some Christians reading this would conclude that it is possible to lose your salvation having once obtained it.

On the other hand, Jesus said, "My sheep hear My voice, and I know them, and they follow Me; and I give eternal life to them, and they shall never perish; and no one shall snatch them out of My hand. My Father, who has given them to Me, is greater than all; and no one is able to snatch them out of the Father's hand" (John 10:27-29). A thorough study of the topic of *assurance of salvation,* comparing Scripture with Scripture, however, indicates that the believer can have assurance that he is saved on the basis of the finished work of Christ.

A further application of this rule is in the use of cross-references in your Bible study. When studying a chapter or a paragraph, the context is the primary place you will look for the interpretation. Cross-references are useful, but you should try to cross-reference the *thought* of the verse rather than just a word or phrase.

For example, in studying the crucifixion of Christ from Matthew 27:27-50, you will be cross-referencing verse 35, "When they had crucified Him, they divided up His garments among themselves, casting lots." Good cross-references would include Psalm 22:18, which is the Old Testament verse quoted here. Also Mark 15:24, Luke 23:34 and John 19:23, 24, all of which are references to the crucifixion from the other Gospels. Secondary cross-references would be Joshua 7:21, I Kings 11:29 and Daniel 7:9, which refer to the word *garment*.

In all of these examples the principle remains the same— let Scripture explain Scripture. The Bible will interpret itself if studied properly.

RULE THREE

Saving faith and the Holy Spirit are necessary for us to understand and properly interpret the Scriptures.

When Jesus was in Galilee by the seaside, the multitudes gathered around Him, drinking in His incredible words as He explained to them the mysteries of the kingdom of heaven. He finished the parable of the sower with these words, "He who has ears, let him hear" (Matthew 13:9). Jesus then interpreted the parable only to His disciples with this explanation: "For the heart of this people has become dull, and with their ears they scarcely hear, and they have closed their eyes lest they should see with their eyes, and hear with their ears, and understand with their heart and turn again, and I should heal them" (Matthew 13:15).

People have two sets of eyes and ears. One set sees and hears things physically, the other spiritually. The Apostle Paul commenting on this said, "In whose case the god of this world has blinded the minds of the unbelieving" (II Corinthians 4:4). The god of this world, Satan, does his utmost to prevent people from perceiving spiritual truth.

The dedicated Christian reads a passage and its truth is self-evident to him. It is so simple and so obvious when he explains it clearly to his non-Christian friend, but that friend fails to grasp its significance. Try as he may, the Christian cannot communicate the simple truth. It is as though there is a barrier of understanding between them.

Through the years Christians have been aware of this problem. Writing to the Corinthians, Paul described it this way: "A natural man does not accept the things of the Spirit of God, for they are foolishness to him, and he cannot understand them, because they are spiritually appraised" (I Corinthians 2:14).

We see a striking example of this at the raising of Lazarus from the dead. Jesus' good friend had been dead four days and decay had already set in. Friends had gathered to console Mary and Martha, the sisters of Lazarus. Then Jesus arrived. The stone was rolled away and Jesus shouted loudly, "Lazarus, come forth" (John 11:43). Still in his graveclothes, Lazarus walked out of the tomb in obedience to the command of Christ.

As John records this event, he says, "Many therefore of the Jews, who had come to Mary and beheld what He had done, believed in Him. But some of them went away to the Pharisees, and told them the things which Jesus had done. Therefore the chief priests and the Pharisees convened a council" (John 11:45-47). Some saw it as it was, a miracle of God. Others viewed this same event with entirely different eyes. They saw it as a threat to their own beliefs, goals and objectives.

It is easy to stand aghast at such crass unbelief. But before we judge too harshly, we might remind ourselves that this is the result of a spiritual battle. Satan seeks to blur our spiritual vision in like manner. The Bible says, "Now we have received, not the spirit of the world, but the Spirit who is from God, that we might know the things freely given to us by God" (I Corinthians 2:12). We must study the Bible with a deep sense of dependence on the Holy Spirit, realizing that He is the One who "will guide you into all the truth" (John 16:13).

It is possible to claim the Bible as your authority and still be spiritually blind. You may have had the experience of being approached by someone from the Jehovah's Witnesses, the Mormons or some other cult. These people are quick to tell you that their faith is based on the Bible, but you do not have to speak with them long before you realize that they have failed to interpret the Bible properly. Rather, they have twisted its meaning to substantiate their own positions.

This problem of using the Bible as your authority while being blinded to its true meaning is not limited to the cults. Many of the worst atrocities through the centuries have been committed in the name of Christ. In the early 12th century, in response to the church's call, thousands gathered under the banner of the cross to free the Holy Land (Palestine) from the Muslims. It was not uncommon for the zealots in these crusades (as they were called) to massacre whole communities of Jews and pagans, even impaling infants by throwing them into the air and catching them on their spears.

During the Civil War in America the Bible was used both to denounce and to support slavery. It is reported that one of Abraham Lincoln's generals said to him during the fierce conflict, "I hope God is on our side."

The president replied, "Sir, I am not half as concerned that God is on our side as I am that we are on God's side."

Seeing things from God's point of view is a ministry of the Holy Spirit to those who have not only trusted Him for salvation but for enlightenment as well. Though being a Christian is no guarantee that you will accurately interpret every passage in the Bible, it is foundational for properly understanding spiritual truth.

RULE FOUR

Interpret personal experience in the light of Scripture and not Scripture in the light of personal experience.

As you read through the New Testament, you discover that it contains two main types of literature— narrative and instructional or teaching. (Most of Revelation and parts of the gospels can be classified as prophetic.) The narrative portions trace the life of our Lord Jesus in the four gospels and the history of the early church in the Book of Acts. The letters or epistles are largely written to instruct members of these early churches on how to live the Christian life.

When studying the instructional portions you discover the writer does not say that because such and such a thing happened, therefore this must be true. Rather, he asserts just the opposite. Because this is true, a particular thing happened. For example, the New Testament does not teach that because Jesus rose from the dead He is therefore the Son of God. Rather, because He is the Son of God, He rose from the dead.

The events that unfold throughout the Bible are interpreted on the basis of what God states to be true and never vice versa. We do not conclude that the world was wicked because God destroyed it with a flood in the days of Noah. Rather, the Bible says that because the world was wicked God said He would destroy it and did.

Throughout the Book of Acts the narrative of what happened in the lives of first century believers unfolds. You do not draw doctrinal conclusions from these events unless they include preaching. Rather, you interpret these events in the light of the doctrinal passages. There are several instances when people in the Acts record encountered the Holy Spirit. When you analyze all the varied experiences, it becomes obvious that you cannot form doctrine from these encounters. On the Day of Pentecost Peter and the disciples spoke in tongues, and people of different language groups were all able to understand the Gospel in their own languages. "They were amazed and marveled, saying, 'Why, are not all these who are speaking Galileans? And how is it that we each hear them in our own language to which we were born?'" (Acts 2:7, 8)

When Peter went to Samaria to look in on the ministry of Philip, the new converts had not yet received the Holy Spirit. "Then they began laying their hands on them, and they were receiving the Holy Spirit" (Acts 8:17). There is no mention of any speaking in tongues following this occurrence.

After Paul's conversion on the road to Damascus, Ananias came to him and laid hands on him. Paul was filled with the Holy Spirit and was baptized (Acts 9:17-19).

In the city of Ephesus Paul met some men who had been baptized only "unto John's baptism"—a baptism of repentance. Paul preached Jesus to them, and they believed and were baptized. "When Paul had laid his hands upon them, the Holy Spirit came on them, and they began speaking with tongues and prophesying" (Acts 19:6). We are not told what language these men spoke, but it probably was different from that spoken at Pentecost. The situation was different. It was most likely an unknown tongue, requiring an interpreter such as Paul mentions in his letter to the Corinthians (I Corinthians 14).

The teaching portions of the New Testament speak about the use of tongues by believers. The significant passage on this teaching is I Corinthians 12—14. Note that this passage addresses itself to the use and control of tongues without mentioning the practice of tongues as in Acts. In other words, Paul says, "Here is the correct doctrine regarding tongues—make sure your own experience complies with it."

He does not say that because a certain phenomenon was experienced in the church, a certain doctrinal truth may be drawn from it.

Your personal experiences—whatever they may be— must be taken to the Scriptures and interpreted. Never the other way around. "Because I have had this experience, the following must be true" is not sound procedure in interpreting the Bible.

None of this suggests that there is no value in experience. Quite the contrary. Experience attests to the validity of the doctrine. The resurrection of Jesus Christ substantiates the fact that He is the Son of God. You know that your salvation is true because of what you have experienced. But you do not form the doctrine of salvation on the basis of your experience. You take your experience to the Scriptures to find out what has taken place in your life.

We often see in the Bible that a statement is made and an experience follows to prove its validity. For example, we find the following test to see if the man claiming to be a prophet really is one: "When a prophet speaks in the name of the Lord, if the thing does not come about or come true, that is the thing which the Lord has not spoken. The prophet has spoken it presumptuously; you shall not be afraid of him" (Deuteronomy 18:22).

Ahaziah, the son of Ahab and Jezebel, was king over Israel, the northern kingdom. Because of his sin, Elijah the prophet prophesied that he would die. King Ahaziah sent soldiers to arrest Elijah. "And Elijah answered and said to the captain of fifty, 'If I am a man of God, let fire come down from heaven and consume you and your fifty.' Then fire came down from heaven and consumed him and his fifty" (II Kings 1:10). Elijah's prophetic statement was followed by its fulfillment, proving that Elijah was a true prophet of God. His statement was followed by the experience.

Personal experience is an important part of the Christian life, but you must be careful to keep it in its proper place. Though you learn from experience, you do not judge the Bible on the basis of it.

It is easy to forget this in so many areas in life. For example, suppose you have had difficulty with deficit spending. The Lord speaks to you about this and you feel He would have you abolish all forms of buying on credit. You work hard, economize and pay off all your creditors. This revolutionizes your life. You are now free from debt and convinced that you should never return to installment buying. Up to this point all is well.

But then you go one step further and suggest that anyone owning credit cards or buying on time is violating a biblical command. To prove your point you quote, "Owe nothing to anyone" (Romans 13:8). You have now broken this important rule of interpretation. You have interpreted the Bible in the light of your own experience and demanded that others should follow this interpretation.

The Scriptures blend beautifully with life's experiences. The more time you spend in Bible study, the more this truth becomes imprinted in your life. It seems that the biblical authors had *you* in mind when they penned their words, so pointed and alive are the applications.

It is precisely for this reason that you must exercise care in not reversing this rule. You allow the Word of God to interpret and shape your experiences rather than interpreting Scripture from your experiences.

RULE FIVE

Biblical examples are authoritative only when supported by a command.

As you read through the Bible it becomes obvious that you are not to follow the example of every person you meet. You need not follow the example of Moses and confront the leaders of Egypt. You are not to follow the example of King David and commit adultery and murder. Nor are you to follow the example of the Apostle Peter in denying Christ.

These illustrations may seem to be oversimplified, but the Bible is full of many examples that *are* worthy of imitation. Are you not obligated to follow these? Yes, if the example illustrates a biblical command. No, if the example is not supported by such a command.

Jesus Christ is the perfect Man. If ever there is a life worth copying it is His. As we look at His perfect life, if we find it is not necessary to follow all His examples, it will logically follow that this will be true for the rest of the Bible.

Jesus wore a long robe and sandals. Usually He walked. When He did ride, it was on a donkey. He never married and never left the country of His birth (except as an infant when His parents fled to Egypt to escape from King Herod and a brief visit to Syro-Phoenicia). It becomes immediately apparent that you are not expected to follow His example in areas such as these.

For instance, to follow Jesus' example in His remaining single would mean that Christians are not to marry; yet the Bible has a great deal to say about the marital relationship, commending it highly and using it as an illustration of the whole Christ-Church relationship.

Jesus was a man of great love and compassion. You know you are to follow His example in this because He said, "A new commandment I give to you, that you love one another, even as I have loved you, that you also love one another. By this all men will know that you are My disciples, if you have love for one another" (John 13:34, 35).

Examples from the life of Jesus or from the lives of His followers that are *not* supported by commands do have some value:

1. A biblical example can verify what you feel the Lord is leading you to do. You may feel, for instance, that God would have you remain single the rest of your life. Since most people marry, you may feel pressure from others in this direction. But your conviction that the Lord would have you never marry is biblically supported by the fact that Jesus never married.

2. A biblical example can be a rich source of application for your life. Suppose you are reading the Gospel of Mark and pause to meditate on this account, "In the early morning, while it was still dark, He [Jesus] arose and went out and departed to a lonely place, and was praying there" (Mark 1:35). After thought and prayer you feel the Lord would have you spend time with Him each day early in the morning. This would be an appropriate application and would undoubtedly benefit your spiritual life.

To take this application, however, and try to apply it to other people would be taking an example from the Bible and treating it as a command. The Scripture does command us to pray; Paul urged, "Pray without ceasing" (I Thessalonians 5:17). And the Bible does exhort us to spend time in the Word, "Let the Word of Christ richly dwell within you, with all wisdom teaching and admonishing one another with psalms and hymns and spiritual songs, singing with thankfulness in your hearts to God" (Colossians 3:16). No command of Scripture says that this should be done early in the morning, even though this is when Jesus did it, and may be the best time for you.

Each individual must draw his own application from those biblical examples that are not followed by a command. The commandments of the Bible are, of course, authoritative for all people. But biblical examples, unless supported by a command, are not.

* * *

A corollary to this principle is also true:
The believer is free to do anything that the Bible does not prohibit.

An obvious example of this principle may be seen in the present-day activities of the church. A local congregation may build a new sanctuary, develop a large Sunday School, begin a Boy's Brigade work or start a Christian day school. The Scriptures do not have examples of these, much less commands to do them, yet such actions are entirely permissible. The Bible sets boundaries on what *cannot* be done, not on what can be done. All things are lawful unless specifically prohibited.

Such a clear prohibition applies in the area of premarital and extramarital sex. Paul says that such people "shall not inherit the kingdom of God" (see I Corinthians 6:9).

The Holy Spirit uses the Bible to guide and direct our lives. As we follow His leading and expose ourselves to the great truths of the Scriptures, we take upon ourselves more and more the character of Jesus Christ. The Bible calls this process sanctification. And in sanctification the Lord gives us great freedom—freedom in the exciting adventure of becoming Christlike.

As we study the Bible, we must exercise care that we do not restrict this freedom either for ourselves or for others. To quote the great Puritan divines of a by-gone day, "The Bible is our only rule for faith and practice."

RULE SIX

The primary purpose of the Bible is to change our lives, not increase our knowledge.

When He superintended the writing of the Bible, the Holy Spirit intended that we who read the Scriptures learn and apply what is taught. The Scriptures themselves state this as their intended purpose.

When Paul wrote his first epistle to the Corinthians he drew from the experience of Israel during the Exodus to make his point. Israel lusted in the wilderness for things they didn't have. Commenting on this to the church in Corinth, Paul says, "These things happened as examples for us, that we should not crave evil things, as they also craved" (I Corinthians 10:6).

Two of the ways you can learn a lesson are through personal experiences and through the experiences of others. Some lessons in life you can learn only by living through them. But some lessons are too expensive to learn that way. The wise person will learn them by observing the lives of others.

The unbelief of Israel during the Exodus cost that nation 40 wasted years of wandering in the wilderness. Paul says to the Corinthians that God recorded this for us so that we would not make the same tragic mistakes. In a most remarkable way the Lord shows us in the pages of the Bible the failures and shortcomings (as well as the strengths) of His people so that we can learn from them. "Learn from their strengths and avoid their weaknesses," seems to be the Holy Spirit's message to us.

We must understand before we can apply, but understanding without application does not make a person godly. Satan knows the Bible well. No doubt he could pass any examination in theology offered him. He has even memorized Scripture, which he demonstrated when he quoted from the Psalms during the temptation of Jesus.

"Jesus was led up by the Spirit into the wilderness to be tempted by the devil. And after He had fasted forty days and forty nights, He then became hungry. And the tempter came and said to Him, 'If You are the Son of God, command that these stones become bread.'

"But He answered and said, 'It is written, "Man shall not live on bread alone, but on every word that proceeds out of the mouth of God." '

"Then the devil took Him into the holy city; and he stood Him on the pinnacle of the temple, and said to Him, 'If You are the Son of God throw Yourself down; for it is written, "He will give His angels charge concerning You; and on their hands they will bear You up, lest You strike Your foot against a stone" [Psalm 91:11, 12].'

"Jesus said to him, 'On the other hand, it is written, "You shall not tempt the Lord your God." '

"Again, the devil took Him to a very high mountain, and showed Him all the kingdoms of the world, and their glory; and he said to Him, 'All these things will I give You, if You fall down and worship me.'

"Then Jesus said to him, 'Begone, Satan! For it is written, "You shall worship the Lord you God, and serve Him only." ' Then the devil left Him; and behold, angels came and began to minister to Him" (Matthew 4:1-11).

"The demons also believe, and shudder," is the way James put it (James 2:19). The Bible was not given to us so that we could be as smart as the devil; it was given to us so that we could become as holy as God. Peter has written, "He has granted to us His precious and magnificent promises, in order that by them you might become partakers of the divine nature, having escaped the corruption that is in the world by lust" (II Peter 1:4).

Paul advised Timothy, "All Scripture is inspired by God and profitable for teaching, for reproof, for correction, for training in righteousness; that the man of God may be adequate, equipped for every good work" (II Timothy 3:16, 17). All Scripture was given with this end in mind—that it shape our lives. You must be careful, though, when seeking to apply "all Scripture" to remember two things. They may be stated as corollaries to this rule.

* * *

1. Some passages are not to be applied in the same way they were applied at the time they were written.

Suppose you are reading through the Book of Leviticus, seeking to make an application to your life, and you read, "This is the law of the guilt offering; it is most holy. In the place where they slay the burnt offering they are to slay the guilt offering, and he shall sprinkle its blood around on the altar" (Leviticus 7:1, 2). A wrong application would be to do the same thing the Old Testament priests did: offer an animal sacrifice.

The New Testament tells us that Jesus Christ "abolished in His flesh the enmity, even the law of commandments contained in ordinances" (Ephesians 2:15, KJV). You might possibly apply this Leviticus passage by purposing to reflect on how great a price the Saviour paid to have every one of your sins forgiven, using the Old Testament sacrificial system as a point of reference.

The Bible offers another possible application: "Through Him then let us continually offer up a sacrifice of praise to God, that is, the fruit of lips that give thanks to His name. And do not neglect doing good and sharing; for with such sacrifices God is pleased" (Hebrews 13:15, 16).

2. When you apply a passage it must be in keeping with a correct interpretation.

For example, our Lord is coming down from the Mount of Transfiguration when He meets some of His disciples trying to heal an epileptic (Matthew 17:14-16). Since they are unable to do it, the boy's father turns to Jesus for help. Jesus casts out the unclean spirit and the frustrated disciples later ask why they were unable to do it. Jesus replies, "Because of the littleness of your faith; for truly I say to you, if you have faith as a mustard seed, you shall say to this mountain, 'Move from here to there,' and it shall move; and nothing shall be impossible to you" (17:20).

If you were burdened for a loved one who had a terminal disease, you might read this passage, and, wanting to make an application, reason that only your lack of faith was keeping you from healing him. You try to heal him, but the person dies. So you blame yourself and think, *Maybe it is because of sin in my life that I was unable to heal him.*

Probably sin and unbelief were not your problem. You simply misinterpreted the passage. Earlier, Jesus had specifically instructed His disciples, "Heal the sick, raise the dead, cleanse the lepers, cast out demons; freely you received, freely give" (Matthew 10:8). They were rebuked for their lack of faith because they had been commanded by the Lord to heal and had been endowed with appropriate power to do so. God did not give such a specific command to you.

Every part of the Bible is applicable to you. Correct interpretation, however, is essential before you seek to make application. Failure to do so may lead to unnecessary misunderstanding and heartache. Take care to interpret the passage correctly, then prayerfully make the application.

RULE SEVEN

Each Christian has the right and responsibility to investigate and interpret the Word of God for himself.

This principle was one of the undergirding foundations of the Protestant Reformation in the 16th Century. For hundreds of years, people had depended on the church to do the studying and interpreting of the Scriptures for them. There were no translations of the Bible in the language of the people. When attempts were made to produce such translations, the church strongly suppressed them.

Today there are a multitude of available translations and paraphrases, making access to the Bible easy for anyone who can read. Yet our generation seems to be producing biblically illiterate people. Even among conscientious Christians the Bible is little more than a devotional book in which to "meet" God. Digging for the great truths of the Bible is left for the theologians and other "experts." It is as though we were returning to the days before the Reformation.

The presence of the Holy Spirit and the ability of language to communicate truth combine to give you all you need to study and interpret the Bible for yourself. In the ministry of our Lord Jesus, He rebuked the Jews of His day for their inability to understand who He was. He attributed this failure directly to their ignorance of the Scriptures. "You search the Scriptures, because you think that in them you have eternal life; and it is these that bear witness of Me" (John 5:39).

Later Jesus said that a distinguishing mark of one who is His disciple is that he "continue in My Word" (John 8:31, KJV). All through the epistles this theme is picked up and emphasized. "Let the Word of Christ richly dwell within you, with all wisdom teaching and admonishing one another with psalms and hymns and spiritual songs, singing with thankfulness in your hearts to God" (Colossians 3:16), Paul admonished the believers at Colosse. To his son in the faith he put it this way, "Be diligent to present yourself approved to God as a workman who does not need to be ashamed, handling accurately the Word of truth" (II Timothy 2:15).

In-depth study will not always give you the answers you seek. Frequently you will encounter a truth whose depths elude you. And your mind is so constituted that it can ask more questions than it can answer. Bible study will not answer all of your questions. Answers to some questions will come later, like finding the missing piece in a jigsaw puzzle. Some will never be answered this side of heaven. An appreciation for the mysteries in the Christian faith is in itself a sign of maturity.

When your private interpretation leads you to a conclusion different from the historic meaning men of God have given to the passage, an amber light of caution should flash in your mind. Any conclusion you come to that differs from the historic evangelical position should be considered suspect. More often than not, after further study, you will find that your interpretation was in error.

If you are blessed with a pastor and Sunday School that faithfully expound the Bible, you have a rich heritage indeed. This, however, could easily lull you into relying on others to feed you rather than disciplining yourself to feed your own soul. It should not be an either/or proposition, but a both/and. You should maintain a balance between being taught by others and feeding yourself. The more skilled you become in personal Bible study, the more you will rely on your pastor as a check on how you interpreted the passage rather then as the primary source of your scriptural intake.

Even when you learn spiritual truth from the preaching of

others, you are responsible for weighing this truth with what you find in your own Bible study and for forming your own convictions. This is what made the Berean Church noble in the eyes of Luke. Notice what he says about them. "These [the Bereans] were more noble-minded than those in Thessalonica, for they received the Word with great eagerness, examining the Scriptures daily, to see whether these things were so" (Acts 17:11).

Underline the words *great eagerness*. The noble Bereans received Paul's teaching with openness and attentiveness. But they did not stop there. When Paul was through preaching they examined "the Scriptures daily, to see whether those things were so." What a combination! Listen attentively to the Word and then study the Bible to form your own convictions.

When you accept an idea simply because someone else tells you it is so, you short-circuit the process, even if what you are told is accurate and worthy of belief. You have believed the right thing for the wrong reason. It has not yet become your conviction. This is why so many Christians fall prey to heretical groups such as the Jehovah's Witnesses and the Mormons.

A different illustration will make the same point. A Christian friend encourages you to memorize Scripture. You do it because he tells you to do it. You have no conviction of your own that you should do it, and it is hard work. After an enthusiastic beginning you let it slip. Unfaithful in your review, you soon forget the verses you have memorized, and in discouragement you quit. Only if you are *convinced* God wants you to memorize, will you jump the hurdles of discouragement and go on to victory.

As we have already seen, God commands us to spend time with Him in the Scriptures. Scripture memory, however, is a *method* of getting into the Word. You may not necessarily be convinced of the method that others use; in that case you must go before the Lord and ask Him *how* He wants you to go about investigating and interpreting the Bible.

A method is a vehicle for digging into the Word. The process of digging into Scripture and coming to your own conclusion is what changes mere beliefs into rock-ribbed convictions. Involvement in this process is not only your right as a child of God, but also your solemn responsibility.

RULE EIGHT

Church history is important but not decisive in the interpretation of Scripture.

In the introduction to this book we compared the authority of *reason* and *tradition* to the authority of *Scripture.* Though all three authorities are important and have their proper place, reason and tradition must yield to Scripture. When there is disagreement among the three types of authority, Scripture must be the final court of appeal. It is the *final* authority.

There is a proper place for reason and tradition, and here we want to examine the place of tradition or church history. For the sake of simplicity we will equate the two.

Many doctrines considered essential by evangelicals are implied in the Scriptures. Because they are implied and not explicitly stated there was a time when they were quite controversial. We are indebted to church history for the fact that such issues are settled.

One such doctrine is the deity of Jesus Christ, that is, that He is coeternal with the Father, that He is God. There never was a time when He was not. He is "very God of very God." This doctrine is biblical. It is taught in several places in the Bible. The prologue to the Gospel of John gives a clear example, "In the beginning was the Word, and the Word was with God, and the Word was God . . . and the Word became flesh, and dwelt among us" (John 1:1, 14). The correct interpretation of this and other related passages came with the maturing of the church. We are indebted to church history which records what the believers of past ages hammered out on the anvil of soul-searching, scriptural investigation and debate.

* * *

A corollary to this rule is:

The church does not determine what the Bible teaches; the Bible determines what the church teaches.

The interpretations of the church have authority only insofar as they are in harmony with the teachings of the Bible as a whole. History was not meant to be decisive in the interpretation of Scripture, for there have been times when the church has not been true to the Word of God. In early medieval times it taught the celibacy of the clergy, that priests could never marry. Later medieval times exalted Mary to a position equal with God. These were determinations of the church, not the Bible. The interpretations of the church must be carefully studied and evaluated in light of what the Bible teaches.

Having voiced this caution, however, we still must not overlook the importance of church history. It can provide a check and balance for you in your own study of the Bible. Charles H. Spurgeon, the famous English preacher, is reported to have said, "It seems odd that certain men who talk so much of what the Holy Spirit reveals to them should think so little of what He revealed to others." There is an important place for commentaries and the creeds in forming doctrine. God's saints of the past have a great deal to say to us today, if only we will listen.

Many evangelicals overreact by refusing to consider any source other than the Bible, and not without reason. The attack on the Word of God has been fierce these past decades. Many of the historic creeds of the church have been revised and watered down to include the philosophical biases of the day. You must be careful to maintain balance here. Learn from history and recognize its important contribution while remembering that the Bible is the final arbitrator in all matters pertaining to faith and practice.

RULE NINE

The promises of God throughout the Bible are available to the Holy Spirit for the believers of every generation.

The promises of God found in the Bible are a means by which God reveals His will to men. In saying this, we must acknowledge that claiming promises is a subjective thing. For that matter, so is using any method to determine God's will for one's life.

Many people become uneasy when biblical promises are used, partly because they are so often misused. A not-so-funny caricature of a person claiming a biblical promise shows him opening a Bible with eyes closed and placing his finger in the middle of the page. Where the finger rests is God's promise to him.

The problem is not in claiming a promise per se, but in determining the will of God. Use the same caution in claiming God's promises that you use when you determine the will of God. The Lord requires all of us to act on the basis of faith. The promises are given as a valuable tool in helping us respond properly.

Claiming the promises of God is a specific form of application. Note the emphasis that was given to application in Rule Six: *The primary purpose of the Bible is to change our lives, not increase our knowledge* (page 34). Just as it is essential that you interpret the passage properly before applying it, so also it is essential to interpret the promise properly before claiming it.

If you are not careful about what the passage says, all sorts of fanciful interpretations can follow. For example, you may desire leadership from the Lord for your life. After much prayer you claim Isaiah 30:21, "Your ears will hear a word behind you, 'This is the way, walk in it,' whenever you turn to the right or to the left." You are asking the Lord to tell you when to turn to the right and when to turn to the left. From now on you are going to get your directions straight from God, for is this not what He has promised?

As you study the context of Isaiah 30:21, you learn that the word spoken from behind you is from your teachers. From God, yes, but through your teachers. Failure to interpret the verse properly can lead you to misunderstand how God wants to lead you.

It is permissible to claim a promise outside of its historical context as long as you are true to what the passage says and means. For example, let us say you are surrounded by adverse circumstances and accused falsely. You pray, asking the Lord for guidance. He leads you to claim Exodus 14:14, "The Lord will fight for you while you keep silent." This promise was originally given to Moses when Israel was surrounded by adverse circumstances. But with this promise God quiets your heart and you wait on Him to work things out.

The Bible gives numerous encouragements to claim the promises in this manner. Peter, exhorting his flock to a devout and holy life, said, "His divine power has granted to us everything pertaining to life and godliness, through the true knowledge of Him who called us by His own glory and excellence. For by these He has granted to us His precious and magnificent promises, in order that by them you might become partakers of the divine nature, having escaped the corruption that is in the world by lust" (II Peter 1:3, 4). The psalmist expressed it this way: "The counsel of the Lord stands forever, the plans of His heart from generation to generation" (Psalm 33:11).

A proper attitude is important as you approach the promises. The Lord has given them to you to help you do His will. Yet so often people use them to try to get God to do their will. The Bible says, "Until now you have asked for nothing in My name; ask, and you will receive, that your joy may be made full" (John 16:24). Jesus Himself made that promise. You are in love with someone and want to marry that person. Or you and your spouse want a child. So you claim this promise, but don't get your wish. Why? Possibly because God did not give you that particular promise. You took it. But God is not your servant; you are His. You defeat the purpose of the promises when you make them self-serving.

A promise is God's commitment to do something, and requires your response of faith in the form of obedience. Sometimes that obedience means patiently waiting on the Lord to do what He promises. Another time it may mean launching out into the unknown or taking great risks. God's promises form the foundation for the expression of faith. Without the promise you have no basis for asking. With the promise you respond by faith. Faith is always active, never passive. As you, by faith, respond to God's promise, His will is performed and He is glorified.

Suppose you respond to the promise and it is not fulfilled? It appears that God did not do what He promised. To what conclusions can you then come? Three possibilities are:

1. God let you down. He failed to carry out His end of the bargain. If this is so, the Bible is not trustworthy; it is not worth following Christ; in short, the God of the Scriptures does not exist. For God Himself said, "God is not a man, that He should lie, nor a son of man, that He should repent; has He said, and will He not do it? Or has He spoken, and will He not make it good?" (Numbers 23:19)

Though we list "God let you down" as a possible conclusion, it is in fact an impossibility. It is an impossibility because God promises He will *never* let us down. Paul was speaking to Timothy when he said, concerning the reliability of God, "He remains faithful; for He cannot deny Himself"

(II Timothy 2:13). We can rule out this possibility simply because God *always* does what He promises.

2. You misclaimed the promise. This is an unpleasant possibility, but a real one. If you have ever had the misfortune of claiming a promise God never intended for you to claim, don't think that you are alone. Many have done it. It usually happens when your motives become confused. Was the promise claimed with a sincere desire to do God's will and nothing else? Or was what you wanted interjected somewhere along the line?

If you felt you sought only to please God, then you should suspend judgment as to what happened. Even Paul wasn't always sure of his own motives. He said, "To me it is a very small thing that I should be examined by you, or by any human court; in fact, I do not even examine myself. I am conscious of nothing against myself, yet I am not by this acquitted; but the One who examines me is the Lord. Therefore, do not go on passing judgment before the time, but wait until the Lord comes who will both bring to light the things hidden in the darkness and disclose the motives of men's hearts; and then each man's praise will come to him from God" (I Corinthians 4:3-5).

God knows your heart and will someday reveal what happened. You may have misappropriated the promise, but a third choice still remains.

3. It will be fulfilled at a later time and/or in a way you don't expect. God promised Abraham that his descendants would be as numerous as the stars in the heavens. He and Sarah were still waiting patiently for its fulfillment after she had passed through menopause and Abraham was about 100 years old. They had even tried to help God fulfill His promise, but all in vain. Abraham had a child by Sarah's handmaiden Hagar, but this wasn't what God had in mind. Old age had come to this family and still there were no

children. The natural fulfillment of the promise was not to be. God wanted it fulfilled in a *supernatural* way.

Speaking of this, the author of Hebrews says, "All these, having gained approval through their faith, *did not receive what was promised"* (Hebrews 11:39). Here were God's heroes of the faith who never lived to see God's promises fulfilled. God fulfilled them in another generation. They did not "abandon ship" and give up. They held tenaciously to the promises and trusted God to fulfill them in His own way.

God has not let you down, and you may not have misclaimed the promise. The Lord may fulfill it in a way and at a time you don't suspect. God's will according to God's timetable is what all of us should be trying to follow.

It may be helpful to consider the two types of promises found in the Bible:

1. *General Promises.* These are promises given by the Holy Spirit to every believer. When they were penned by the author no individual person or period of time was intended. Rather they are *general,* that is, intended for all people in all generations.

An example of this type of promise is: "If we confess our sins, He is faithful and righteous to forgive us our sins and to cleanse us from all unrighteousness" (I John 1:9). This promise was true for the people to whom John was writing, and it is equally true for you today. There are many such promises throughout the Bible.

2. *Specific Promises.* These are promises given by the Holy Spirit to specific individuals on specific occasions. Like the general promises, specific promises are available to you as the Holy Spirit may lead. The difference is that specific promises must be given expressly to you by the Holy Spirit as they were given to the original recipients. In this sense they are much more subjective than general promises. You can *know* that *all* general promises are given to you, and

to everyone else. Specific promises, however, are *available* to you, but don't become yours unless specially given to you by God. Specific promises are most often given for guidance and for blessing.

The Holy Spirit may choose to give you a specific promise to help you determine His will. That is, when He wants to guide you in a particular direction. For example, "Your gates will be open continually; they will not be closed day or night, so that men may bring to you the wealth of the nations, with their kings led in procession" (Isaiah 60:11).

As you pray over this verse and become increasingly convinced that the Lord wants you to claim it for your life, you may decide to open your home 24 hours a day for all whom the Lord sends you. The promise was originally given to the Messiah, but the Spirit of God can give it to you for your ministry.

On their first missionary journey, Paul and Barnabas were opposed by the Jews while they ministered the Word in Antioch of Pisidia. They felt God was calling them to the Gentiles, and to substantiate this leading Paul quoted from Isaiah, "For thus has the Lord commanded us, 'I have placed You as a light for the Gentiles, that you should bring salvation to the end of the earth'" (Acts 13:47; see Isaiah 42:6, 7). Paul quoted a messianic verse which the Lord had given him for guidance.

Blessing is the other way specific promises are used. The Holy Spirit may not be seeking to guide you, but simply to reveal the blessing He plans for your life. To illustrate this, let us say your church is without a pastor. The last one you had was unsatisfactory, and the leaders of the congregation have been cautious in calling his successor. Months have gone by and you are concerned that the Lord give you the right pastor. As you pray over the situation, the Lord assures you of His promised blessing with the words, "I will give you shepherds after My own heart, who will feed you on knowledge and understanding" (Jeremiah 3:15).

Because specific promises are subjective, if you have been a Christian for only a short time, it is best to stay with the *general* promises found in the New Testament for the first couple of years. When you do feel ready to claim specific promises, then you should follow certain guidelines:

1. The spirit of God gives them to individual Christians at particular times in their lives as He chooses.

2. Promises are often conditional and the condition is obedience. You can detect the condition by the presence of the little word *if* in the verse or context.

3. The Holy Spirit of God is sovereign. "The counsel of the Lord stands forever, the plans of His heart from generation to generation" (Psalm 33:11). He can speak from any passage to any person at any time.

4. Do not prejudge the Lord as to when and how the promise will be fulfilled in your life.

5. God gives His promises to make you more dependent on Him, not independent. Claim them in a spirit of dependence and humility.

6. God's intent is to glorify Himself by giving you promises. Never fail to give Him the glory when the promise is fulfilled.

One further caution is in order before we draw this to a close. When you claim a promise from the Bible, you are determining the will of God in that particular matter. This in turn cuts you off from any further counsel, for who wishes to counsel against the will of God? For example, let us say you are praying and seeking counsel about changing jobs. You claim a promise from the Word that in effect tells you, "It is the will of God to make the change." At that point no further counsel is needed. Now you need to act on what God has said.

In doing this, however, you place full responsibility for the decision on your own shoulders. You have determined God's will by yourself. This is not bad, unless you have misclaimed the promise. The caution comes in making sure you allow for sufficient time and prayer to make the promise a conviction in your soul that this is truly what God wants.

3 Grammatical Principles of Interpretation

Grammatical principles deal with the very words of the text. How should you understand the words and sentences in the passages under study? What are the ground rules to remember when dealing with the text? These principles answer those questions.

* * *

RULE TEN

Scripture has only one meaning and should be taken literally.

In the everyday affairs of life, no serious, conscientious person intends what he says or writes to carry a diversity of meanings. Rather, he desires that the true and obvious sense be understood by his hearers or readers. If you were to say to an audience, "I crossed the ocean from the United States to Europe," you wouldn't want them to interpret your statement to mean that you crossed life's difficult waters into the haven of a new experience. Likewise, no journalist would like to write of the famine and suffering of a country such as India and have his words interpreted to mean that the people of India were experiencing a great intellectual hunger.

As ridiculous as this sounds, much of the ecumenical church does precisely that in their interpretation of the Bible. They call it the use of "connotative words." For example, they don't use *reconciliation* in the biblical sense of a man being reconciled to God. They draw the word from biblical passages, give it their meaning and talk about man's reconciliation with man. *Redemption* is not used in the scriptural sense of man being saved from sin and punishment. Rather, they take this word from a Bible text, give it a different "connotation" and suggest that it has to do with sociological and cultural improvements.

In order to communicate, you must assume that (1) the true intent of speech is to convey thought, and that (2) language is a reliable medium of communication.

The literal interpretation in context, therefore, is the only true interpretation. If you don't take a passage literally all sorts of fanciful interpretations may result.

When you encounter a passage in which a literal interpretation is indicated from the context and you elect to give it an other-than-literal interpretation, evaluate your motives carefully. As honestly as you can, answer the following questions:

1. Am I questioning this passage being literal because I do not want to obey it? For example, Paul says, "Let the women keep silent in the churches; for they are not permitted to speak, but let them subject themselves, just as the law also says" (I Corinthians 14:34). Your response is that this was a cultural issue, relevant in its day but not in ours. What led you to that conclusion? A desire *not* to do what the

Bible commands or a sincere desire to please God and keep His commandments? If it is the former, then you are on shaky ground and need to deal with the issue of lordship in your life. If it is the latter, then you are free to pursue your study and see if the rules of interpretation warrant such a conclusion.

2. Am I interpreting this passage literally because it does not fit my preconceived theological bias? An Old Testament incident gives us an example: "Then he [Elisha] went up from there to Bethel; and as he was going up by the way, young lads came up from the city and mocked him and said to him, 'Go up, you baldhead; go up, you baldhead!' When he looked behind him and saw them, he cursed them in the name of the Lord. Then two female bears came out of the woods and tore up forty-two lads of their number" (II Kings 2:23, 24). Your immediate reaction may be that God could never allow such an incident to occur. God is just not like that! Once again you must pause and analyze your motives. Is your response to this passage born out of an embarrassment over what God is reported to have done? If your conclusion is the result of your trying to get God to behave the way you think He should, then again your whole approach to interpretation is wrong. You are God's servant. Your task is to understand who He is and what He expects. The objective of your Bible study is not to confirm *your* ideas of what God is like.

The application of the rules of interpretation must always be founded on a correct motive.

So determine what is the usual and ordinary sense of the word or passage and consider it the correct meaning unless the context demands otherwise.

No statement may be considered to have more than one meaning. No word can mean more than one thing as it is used in a passage. The same word may change meaning within the same sentence as it is used more than once, however. An example of this is, "God is Spirit; and those who worship Him must worship in spirit and truth" (John 4:24). *Spirit* is used twice in this verse. The first time it refers to the Holy Spirit for it says, "God is Spirit," and the Holy Spirit is God. The second use of the word *spirit* can be seen from the context to refer, not to God, but to the totality of the inner person—his essential inner being, his very heart. The word *spirit* changes meaning, but the word cannot mean more than one thing at a time. That is, *spirit* as used the first time can *only* mean God. It can never mean anything else.

When a passage or a word appears to have more than one meaning, choose the clearest interpretation. The most obvious meaning is usually the correct meaning.

This rule is frequently broken. For example, in Jesus' feeding of the 5,000, most people reading the account would accept it as meaning what it says. Yet some interpreters would have us believe that the real meaning of the passage is that Jesus drew out of the crowds a latent spirit of generosity. When they saw the boy share his lunch, they followed his example by pulling their meals out from under their robes.

Before we become overly harsh with those who would misuse the Scripture in this way, we should examine our own practices. The Book of Judges relates the story of Jephthah's vow to God. If God would grant him victory, he would offer in sacrifice the first thing he met when returning home. It was his beloved daughter that he met. Jephthah had vowed, "I will offer it up for a burnt offering" (Judges 11:31). Then the record states that he "did to her according to the vow which he had made" (11:39). You can easily become embarrassed by such stories and conclude that they didn't happen *exactly* the way they were written.

The thought of a man offering his own daughter as a

sacrifice to the God of the Scriptures is, to say the least, repugnant. How easy it would be to take the tools of interpretation and draw a different conclusion. As you find yourself yielding to such an urge, remember this important rule of interpretation: *Scripture has only one meaning and should be taken literally.*

RULE ELEVEN

Interpret words in harmony with their meaning in the times of the author.

In the closing days of Jesus' ministry He told several parables about the kingdom of heaven. One of these was the parable of the ten virgins (Matthew 25:1-13). Five were wise because they had sufficient oil for their lamps, and five were foolish because they did not. What was the lamp used for in the ancient wedding feast? What did it look like? These are some questions a student should ask when studying this passage. Here is an example of the need to understand the meaning and use of the word at the time of its writing.

Determining the correct meaning of words found in the Bible is not particularly difficult these days. Many excellent translations are available, and when the meaning of a word is not clear from these, a good Bible dictionary will usually be helpful.

Occasionally the biblical writer will give his own meaning to a particular word. For example, Jesus drove "the changers of money" (John 2:14, KJV) out of the temple. The Jews didn't like this and began arguing with Him. Jesus answered them by saying, "Destroy this temple, and in three days I will raise it up." The Jews then said, "It took forty-six years to build this temple, and will You raise it up in three days?" Jesus, of course, "was speaking of the temple of His body" (John 2:19-21).

John tells us that the temple to which Jesus was referring was His body. Here he gives us the meaning of the word *temple.* Earlier John talked about "changers of money." He did not explain who they were and what they were doing, so you must research the answer to this yourself. By referring to a Bible dictionary or a commentary on the Gospel of John you should find your answer.

Paul interprets the meaning of *me* in his testimony about his own struggles, "For I know that nothing good dwells in me, that is, in my flesh; for the wishing is present in me, but the doing of the good is not" (Romans 7:18). *Me* can refer to the will, the intellect, the spiritual or the physical man. Or it can refer to the total person. Paul limits its use here and tells us its exact meaning.

As you study a passage, never skip over words you do not understand. An erroneous impression as to the meaning of a single word can easily obscure the meaning of the sentence and possibly the whole paragraph. Even words you think you understand, should be investigated.

An example of this is in Proverbs 29:18. The *King James Version* reads, "Where there is no vision, the people perish." The word *vision* is a poor translation. The marginal reading of the *New American Standard Bible* is more accurate in translating it *revelation*. It refers to the need to be under the ministry of the Word for the purpose of moral restraint. An erroneous impression as to the meaning of the word *vision* obscures the meaning of the statement.

As you study a particular word you should determine four things:

1. *Its use by the author.* Exciting word studies in English are possible if you care to do a little digging. If the word is central to the thought of the author throughout the book, it can prove most helpful. For example, the word *sin* is important to the Apostle John. A study of this word as used by him in his first epistle will help you understand the whole letter.

2. *Its relation to its immediate context.* The context will almost always tell you a great deal about the word.

Paul and his companions were ministering in Philippi when he and Silas were arrested, beaten and cast into prison. At midnight while the men were praising God, an earthquake opened the prison doors and it seemed as though all the prisoners had escaped. The jailer was about to commit suicide, but Paul stopped him.

"And he [the jailer] called for lights and rushed in and, trembling with fear, he fell down before Paul and Silas, and after he brought them out, he said, 'Sirs, what must I do to be saved?' And they said, "Believe in the Lord Jesus, and you shall be saved, you and your household'" (Acts 16:29-31).

What did the jailer mean when he used the word *saved?* Was it the same as the meaning given it by Paul in verse 31? Since the task of this book is not the interpretation of certain biblical passages, but the presenting of *ground rules* for interpretation, you will have to study the context of the narrative to answer these questions yourself.

3. *Its current use at the time of writing.* This requires a more technical study. Generally a reliable translation gives you the best meaning of the word, since the best available scholarship in the church has been involved in these translations. If you desire to pursue it further, you can use a good commentary.

4. *Its root meaning.* This final way of studying the meaning of a word is generally for the more advanced student of the Bible. Reference works are available that give you the historical background of words. The most comprehensive work is the English translation of the *Theological Dictionary of the New Testament,* edited by Gerhard Kittel and Gerhard Friedrich (Wm. B. Eerdmans Publishing Co., Grand Rapids, Michigan). Another good reference work is *Word Studies in the New Testament* by Marvin R. Vincent (Eerdmans). A smaller, one-volume work that is excellent is *An Expository Dictionary of New Testament Words* by W. E. Vine (Fleming H. Revell Co., Old Tappan, New Jersey). Determining the root meaning of a word, however, is not the

most important consideration, and you should not be discouraged if you feel it is beyond you.

We have mentioned the existence and blessing of modern translations. Many of them, however, are more paraphrases than accurate translations, and therefore the personal interpretation and bias of the translator is often apparent. As long as the translator or committee are committed to the authority and inspiration of the Scriptures, the danger is not too severe. However, any time the original text is changed for the sake of clarity, a dangerous precedent is being established. An illustration of this is in the *New English Bible's* translation of Genesis 11:1 which begins, "Once upon a time." The Hebrew word is simply *and.* The phrase "once upon a time" is used in fairy tales and suggests to the reader that the story of the building of the Tower of Babel is simply fiction. Whether such a phrase reflects the bias of the translators is a matter of guesswork. Its presence in the Word of God is unfortunate.

The use of modern translations is helpful, but when doing serious study it is best that you stay with one of the reliable translations. These are: The *King James Version* (KJV), the *American Standard Version* (ASV) and the *New American Standard Bible* (NASB).

When interpreting a word or a passage, your goal is to determine the author's meaning when he wrote it. Try to free yourself of any personal bias when studying a passage. Your objective is to understand the thought of the author, not what you think he ought to have said.

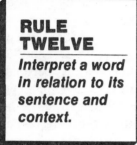

**RULE
TWELVE**

*Interpret a word
in relation to its
sentence and
context.*

We have already noted that it is important to study a word in relation to its immediate context (Rule 11). This is so basic and essential in interpreting the Bible that we list it as a separate rule. The best way to explain it will be to have a series of examples from the Bible when this is necessary.

We begin with the word *faith.* It is an important word in the Bible, especially in the New Testament. Yet we find that it has different meanings in different passages. In one letter Paul says, "They kept hearing, 'He who once persecuted us is now preaching the faith which he once tried to destroy'" (Galatians 1:23). As you study the context you find that *faith* here means, "the doctrine of the Gospel."

When Paul wrote to the Romans he said, "He who doubts is condemned if he eats, because his eating is not from faith; and whatever is not from faith is sin" (Romans 14:23). Here the context leads you to conclude that *faith* means, "conviction that this is what God wants you to do."

In giving advice to his co-laborer Timothy, Paul says, "But the younger widows refuse, for when they have begun to wax wanton against Christ, they will marry; having damnation, because they have cast off their first faith" (I Timothy 5:11, 12, KJV). Here *faith* means, "a pledge or promise made to the Lord." There is, of course, a relationship between the uses of *faith* in these three passages, but the differences are significant enough to note in order to understand what Paul is saying.

A second example is the use of the word *blood.* Luke recorded the message Paul gave to the Athenians on Mars Hill. In it Paul said, "God that made the world and all things therein, seeing that He is Lord of heaven and earth, dwelleth not in temples made with hands; neither is worshiped with men's hands, as though He needed any thing, seeing He giveth to all life, and breath, and all things; and hath made of one blood all nations of men for to dwell on all the face of the earth, and hath determined the times before appointed, and the bounds of their habitation" (Acts 17:24-26, KJV). Paul has said "And hath made of one blood all nations." As you study the context it becomes obvious that *blood* means a group of people.

Paul wrote of the salvation we have through Christ: "In Him we have redemption through His blood, the forgiveness of our trespasses, according to the riches of His grace" (Ephesians 1:7). The word *blood* here refers to the atoning death of Christ.

In another Scripture we read, "Now when these things have been thus prepared, the priests are continually entering the outer tabernacle, performing the divine worship, but into the second only the high priest enters, once a year, not without taking blood, which he offers for himself and for the sins of the people committed in ignorance" (Hebrews 9:6, 7). *Blood* here refers to that fluid which circulates in the veins and arteries of animals that carries nourishment to the body.

Using a different kind of illustration we look at Paul's exhortation to the church at Corinth, "Now concerning the things about which you wrote, it is good for a man not to touch a woman" (I Corinthians 7:1).

Some use this verse to support the idea that a man ought never even to touch a woman in any kind of bodily contact. The context, however, talks about the need to abstain from sexual immorality. In this sense you should not "touch" a woman. It would be erroneous to conclude that a man ought never to touch a woman, like shaking hands with her. In your own study of this passage you might conclude that in order to maintain sexual purity the Lord would have you avoid physical contact with a member of the opposite sex. It would be wrong, however, to make this application normative for all people.

The ancient manuscripts, from which we make our translations of the Bible, have no punctuation marks. There are no periods, commas, paragraphs, verses or chapters. These have since been introduced by the translators for clarity and ease of study. When you do your study it is well to remember this. The context will not always be found within the limits of the verse or chapter. You may have to include verses from the chapter before or after.

This study of the context to determine the proper meaning of a word is one of the most basic and important rules of interpretation. You will find yourself referring to it again and again in your study of the Bible.

RULE THIRTEEN

Interpret a passage in harmony with its context.

Each of the authors of the Bible had a particular reason for writing his book(s). As the author's argument unfolds, there is a logical connection from one section to the next. You must try to find the overall purpose of the book in order to determine the meaning of particular words or passages in the book. These four questions will help:

1. How does the passage relate to the material surrounding it?

2. How does it relate to the rest of the book?

3. How does it relate to the Bible as a whole?

4. How does it relate to the culture and background in which it was written? This fourth question will be handled in a more comprehensive way under Historical Principles of Interpretation (chapter 4), but is important to consider here also.

Answering these four questions becomes especially important when you are trying to interpret a difficult passage. This passage is an example: "No one who abides in Him [Christ] sins; no one who sins has seen Him or knows Him. Little children, let no one deceive you; the one who practices righteousness is righteous, just as He is righteous; the one who practices sin is of the devil; for the devil has sinned from the beginning. The Son of God appeared for this purpose, that He might destroy the works of the devil. No one who is born of God practices sin, because His seed abides in him; and he cannot sin, because he is born of God. By this the children of God and the children of the devil are obvious; any one who does not practice righteousness is not of God, nor the one who does not love his brother" (I John 3:6-10).

When you read this passage by itself, you might conclude that the Christian never sins. Or if he does sin, he cannot be a believer, for "no one who sins has seen Him or knows Him" (verse 6). If this is the correct interpretation, then only Jesus can ever go to heaven, for He is the only sinless person ever to walk the earth—Christian or non-Christian.

What does this passage mean? How should you interpret it? You must interpret it in the light of its context, and answering these four questions will help you do that.

You will see another example of this in the four gospels. They have many things in common, not the least of which is that they all give an account of the life, ministry, crucifixion and resurrection of Jesus Christ. The emphasis of each, however, is different. An understanding of this difference will help you in your study of the parts.

In Matthew we see Jesus as King. He is the fulfillment of all the Old Testament messianic prophecies. Thus you find numerous Old Testament quotations in Matthew.

In Mark Jesus is portrayed as the Servant. The emphasis in this gospel is on the deeds of Christ. No genealogy is given, for who is interested in the genealogy of a servant?

In Luke Jesus is the Son of Man. Here we note the emphasis given to His humanity. His genealogy is traced back to Adam, the first man.

In John we see Jesus as the Son of God. The gospel opens by revealing Him as the eternal Word; He was "in the beginning with God" (John 1:2).

This is not to suggest that the teachings of one gospel cannot be seen in the other three. Quite the contrary. The emphasis of each is different. You need to study each gospel as a whole to catch the panoramic view painted in it. In this way you will see the uniqueness of each, and will be better able to interpret the events and teachings recorded in it.

The importance of this principle cannot be overstated. It is one of the essential rules of interpretation.

RULE FOURTEEN

When an inanimate object is used to describe a living being, the statement may be considered figurative.

The great "I am" passages in John's Gospel illustrate this rule. Jesus said:

"I am the *bread* of life" (John 6:35).

"I am the *light* of the world" (8:12).

"I am the *door* of the sheep" (10:7).

Jesus is neither *bread* nor a *door* in the literal sense. Because an inanimate object such as *bread* is used to describe the Saviour, you can conclude that *bread* must be taken figuratively rather than literally.

Many such examples are found throughout the Bible. The psalmist writes, "The righteous man will flourish like the palm tree, he will grow like a cedar in Lebanon" (Psalm 92:12). The righteous person is likened to a palm or cedar tree. Obviously this is figurative language; an inanimate object is used to describe a living being. It is important to have a clear understanding of the thing on which the figure is based or from which it is borrowed. In this example, your study will be enriched by understanding the characteristics of palm and cedar trees and how they grow.

Another example may be drawn from the great prayer of David in which he asks for forgiveness. "Purify me with hyssop, and I shall be clean; wash me, and I shall be whiter than snow" (Psalm 51:7). What is hyssop and how was it used in those days? A study of the ceremonial purification used in Israel will help you have a fuller appreciation for what David was praying.

Periodically you will come across a passage about which there is disagreement in the church as to its figurative or literal interpretation. For an illustration of this, note Jesus' words regarding the Lord's Supper. "While they were eating, Jesus took some bread, and after a blessing, He broke it and gave it to the disciples, and said, 'Take, eat; this is My body.' And He took a cup and gave thanks, and gave it to them, saying, 'Drink from it, all of you; for this is My blood of the covenant, which is to be shed on behalf of many for forgiveness of sins' " (Matthew 26:26-28).

The Apostle Paul, explaining the meaning of the Lord's Table to the Corinthians, virtually uses the same words. "I received from the Lord that which I also delivered to you, that the Lord Jesus in the night in which He was betrayed took bread; and when He had given thanks, He broke it, and said, 'This is My body, which is for you; do this in remembrance of Me.' In the same way He took the cup also, after supper, saying, 'This cup is the new covenant in My blood; do this, as often as you drink it, in remembrance of Me.' For as often as you eat this bread and drink the cup, you proclaim the Lord's death until He comes" (I Corinthians 11:23-26).

Are the bread and wine in reference to the body and blood of Jesus to be taken figuratively or literally? The church has been and continues to be divided by various interpretations on how the bread and wine are to be understood. You should study the related passages, read what others believe regarding its meaning and why, then form your own convictions. You should, however, allow room for tolerance of the conviction of others regarding the views of the meaning of communion.

* * *

A corollary to this rule is:
When life and action are attributed to inanimate objects, the statement may be considered figurative.

Since this is the same principle viewed another way, one example will bring it into focus.

Micah says, "Listen, you mountains, to the indictment of the Lord, and you enduring foundations of the earth, because the Lord has a case against His people; even with Israel He will dispute" (Micah 6:2). When the writer suggests that the mountains "hear," this should be taken figuratively. He is not suggesting that mountains hear and respond as humans do.

The application of this rule and its corollary in your Bible study should come quite naturally. The context more often than not will tell you immediately whether an inanimate object is used to describe an animate being or is ascribed life and action.

RULE FIFTEEN

When an expression is out of character with the thing described, the statement may be considered figurative.

A group of Jews followed Paul throughout Galatia teaching that Gentile Christians had to be circumcised in order to be saved. They became the object of Paul's wrath in his letter to the Philippians. "Beware of the dogs, beware of the evil workers, beware of the false circumcision; for we are the true circumcision, who worship in the Spirit of God and glory in Christ Jesus and put no confidence in the flesh" (Philippians 3:2, 3). When Paul warns his readers to beware of the dogs, the context does not warrant concluding that he is talking about those four-legged furry animals used as house pets in the western world. He is referring to those who insisted on imposing on Gentile Christians all the ordinances of the Old Testament. Therefore, *dogs* should be interpreted figuratively.

Jesus was en route to Jerusalem, teaching on the way, when some Pharisees warned Him that King Herod was out to kill Him. To this warning Jesus responded, "Go and tell that fox, 'Behold, I cast out demons and perform cures today and tomorrow, and the third day I reach My goal'" (Luke 13:32). *Fox* refers to Herod; we know from the rest of the gospels that Herod isn't the name of a fox, but of an evil king, the one who beheaded John the Baptist. Therefore we can conclude that *fox* must be interpreted in a figurative rather than in a literal way.

Usually the context will tell you whether the statement is figurative or literal, as well as to whom it refers. If you study parallel passages on the subject, they often will help you find the proper interpretation. For example, John the Baptist said concerning Jesus, "Behold, the Lamb of God" (John

1:36). This same phrase is used by Isaiah in his great messianic passage: "He was oppressed and He was afflicted, yet He did not open His mouth; like a lamb that is led to slaughter, and like a sheep that is silent before its shearers, so He did not open His mouth" (Isaiah 53:7). Here the Messiah is referred to as a lamb brought to the slaughter. This and other related passages throughout the Scriptures substantiate the idea that *lamb* is a figurative expression referring to Christ.

At times the same word may be used figuratively, but with different meanings in different places in the Bible. For example, Peter says, "Be of sober spirit, be on the alert. Your adversary, the devil, prowls about like a roaring lion, seeking someone to devour" (I Peter 5:8). Here the context tells you that *lion* refers to Satan.

The Apostle John says, "One of the elders said to me, 'Stop weeping; behold the Lion that is from the tribe of Judah, the Root of David, has overcome so as to open the book and its seven seals'" (Revelation 5:5). Here, too, *lion* is used, but the context suggests that it refers to Christ. Generally, you can arrive at the correct interpretation from the context.

Quite often figurative language is used to describe God. In His endeavor to communicate with man, He describes Himself with human qualities. The chronicler says, "For the eyes of the Lord move to and fro throughout the earth that He may strongly support those whose heart is completely His. You have acted foolishly in this. Indeed, from now on you will surely have wars" (II Chronicles 16:9). The *eyes of the Lord* is a figurative phrase.

Again, God says to His servant Moses, "Then I will take My hand away and you shall see My back, but My face shall not be seen" (Exodus 33:23). The words *hand, back* and *face* are all to be interpreted figuratively.

In order for God to speak to us, He must use human figures and imageries in order to convey the divine truth. Nowhere is this so evident as in the Tabernacle in the Old Testament and the parables of the New Testament. In both situations there is a vehicle (the earthly, human) that bears the spiritual truth. Our understanding of the spiritual world is *analogical.* The fact of God's almightiness is spoken in terms of a right arm because among men the right arm is the stronger of the two and with it the most telling blows are delivered. The fact of pre-eminence is spoken of in terms of sitting at God's right hand because in earthly social situations that is the place of honor. Judgment is spoken of in terms of fire because pain from burning is the most intense known in our more general experience, and the gnawing worm is a symbol of that which is slow, steady, remorseless, and painful. Similarly the glories of heaven are in terms of human experience—costly structures of gold, silver, and jewels, no tears, no death, the tree of life, etc. The question as to whether descriptions of hell and heaven are not literal or symbolic is not the point. In either case they are real, e.g., whether it be literal fire, or that spiritual suffering of which fire is the closest symbol.*

In conclusion, note two important things:

1. A word cannot mean more than one thing at a time. It cannot have a figurative and literal meaning at the same time. When a word is given a figurative meaning, as has been the case in the illustrations used in this rule, the literal meaning of the word is replaced.

2. When at all possible a passage should be interpreted literally. Only if the literal meaning of the word does not fit should it be interpreted figuratively. The literal meaning of a word is always preferred, unless the context makes it impossible.

---

*From *Protestant Biblical Interpretation* by Bernard Ramm. Baker Book House, Grand Rapids, Michigan.

RULE SIXTEEN

The principal parts and figures of a parable represent certain realities. Consider only these principal parts and figures when drawing conclusions.

The ministry of our Lord Jesus was especially rich with parables. He used them to give dynamic and colorful emphasis to spiritual truths. This rule suggests that you should not exceed the intended limits of the parable; don't try to make it say more than it was intended to say. A look at a couple of parables helps us define their limits.

The first is the parable of the sower.

"And when a great multitude were coming together, and those from the various cities were journeying to Him, He spoke by way of a parable:

" 'The sower went out to sow his seed; and as he sowed, some fell beside the road; and it was trampled under foot, and the birds of the air devoured it. And other seed fell on rocky soil, and as soon as it grew up, it withered away, because it had no moisture. And other seed fell among the thorns; and the thorns grew up with it, and choked it out. And other seed fell into the good ground, and grew up, and produced a crop a hundred times as great.'

"As He said these things, He would call out, 'He who has ears to hear, let him hear.'

"And His disciples began questioning Him as to what this parable might be. And He said, 'To you it is granted to know the mysteries of the kingdom of God, but to the rest it is in parables; in order that "seeing they may not see, and hearing they may not understand." Now the parable is this: the seed is the Word of God. And those beside the road are those who have heard; then the devil comes and takes away the Word from their heart, so that they may not believe and be saved.

And those on the rocky soil are those who, when they hear, receive the Word with joy; and these have no firm root; they believe for a while, and in time of temptation fall away. And the seed which fell among the thorns, these are the ones who have heard, and as they go on their way they are choked with worries and riches and pleasures of this life, and bring no fruit to maturity. And the seed in the good ground, these are the ones who have heard the Word in an honest and good heart, and hold it fast, and bear fruit with perseverance'" (Luke 8:4-15).

This is a good parable to study because Jesus gives us the intended interpretation. These verses can be divided into two paragraphs, the parable itself (verses 4-9) and Jesus' interpretation of it (verses 10-15). The principal parts of the parable, as Jesus makes clear in His explanation, are the *seed* and the *types of soil* in which the seed was sown. Though it is often called the parable of the sower, the sower is not the main character. He is incidental to the story.

The purpose of the parable is to illustrate the different types of responses the Word receives when it is proclaimed. As you study the parable, don't extend its purpose beyond the author's intent.

The second parable is Jesus' story of the Good Samaritan.

"A certain man was going down from Jerusalem to Jericho; and he fell among robbers, and they stripped him and beat him, and went off leaving him half dead. And by chance a certain priest was going down on that road, and when he saw him, he passed by on the other side. And likewise a Levite also, when he came to the place and saw him, passed by on the other side. But a certain Samaritan, who was on a journey, came upon him; and when he saw him, he felt compassion, and came to him, and bandaged up his wounds, pouring oil and wine on them; and he put him on his own beast, and brought him to an inn, and took care of him. And on the next day he took out two denarii and gave them to the innkeeper and said, 'Take care of him; and whatever more you spend, when I return, I will repay you' " (Luke 10:30-35).

As you interpret this or any other parable, follow this procedure:

1. Determine the purpose of the parable. In this example the clue is in the opening question. "But wishing to justify himself, he said to Jesus, 'And who is my neighbor?' " (verse 29)

2. Make sure you explain the different parts of the parable in accordance with the main design. In this parable there was the need, there were those who should have met the need but didn't and there was the meeting of the need from an unexpected source. These parts illustrate the duty of universal kindness and doing good.

3. Use only the principal parts of the parable in explaining the lesson. It is when people try to interpret the details that error can easily creep in. Do not make the parable say too much. For example, you may be tempted to suggest that the oil and wine symbolize the Holy Spirit and the blood of Christ (verse 34), the two ingredients necessary for salvation. To do this is to go beyond the intended purpose of the parable.

Determine the main intent of the parable and stay with that. With some parables you will find this easy to do. For example, Jesus asked, "To what shall I compare the kingdom of God? It is like leaven which a woman took and hid in three pecks of meal, until it was all leavened" (Luke 13:20, 21). *Leaven* is a figure which designates a reality, *the kingdom of heaven*. With other parables, you will need to study further before drawing your conclusions.

Each parable has one chief point of comparison. Try to relate this one main point to what the speaker was teaching.

RULE SEVENTEEN

Interpret the words of the prophets in their usual, literal and historical sense, unless the context or manner in which they are fulfilled clearly indicates they have a symbolic meaning. Their fulfillment may be in installments, each fulfillment being a pledge of that which is to follow.

In some ways prophecy is to the Christian what politics is to the secular man, a source of much controversy, heat and emotion. This rule of interpretation is not meant to bias your conviction on prophecy, but simply to establish a guideline for the formation of your convictions. One of the rules already studied states that "Scripture has only one meaning and should be taken literally" (Rule 10, page 53).

Prophecy should be interpreted literally unless the context or some later reference in Scripture indicates otherwise. An example of where a later reference in Scripture indicates that it cannot be taken literally is the prophecy of Malachi regarding the forerunner of Christ. "Behold, I am going to send you Elijah the prophet before the coming of the great and terrible day of the Lord. And he will restore the hearts of the fathers to their children, and the hearts of the children to their fathers, lest I come and smite the land with a curse" (Malachi 4:5, 6).

Malachi says that God will send "Elijah the prophet." When John the Baptist showed up as the forerunner to Jesus Christ, much confusion was generated, which indicates that the people of that day expected prophecy to be fulfilled literally. Jesus, however, said that this prophecy was to have a figurative rather than a literal fulfillment.

On one occasion Jesus stated, "All the prophets and the law prophesied until John. And if you care to accept it, he himself is Elijah, who was to come" (Matthew 11:13, 14). On another occasion, when His disciples asked Him, "Why then do the scribes say that Elijah must come first?" He answered, "Elijah is coming and will restore all things; but I say to you, that Elijah already came, and they did not recognize him, but did to him whatever they wished. So also the Son of Man is going to suffer at their hands." Finally the disciples understood that Jesus called John the Baptist Elijah (Matthew 17:10-13). John the Baptist was the fulfillment of Malachi's prophecy.

Such illustrations are the exception rather than the rule in interpreting prophecy. Most prophecies can and should be interpreted literally. There may be times when you can derive two apparent meanings from a prophecy. Give preference to the one that would have been most obvious to the understanding of the original hearers.

There will also be times when a New Testament writer will ascribe to an Old Testament passage a prophetic interpretation when the Old Testament passage does not appear to be prophetic. You will find an example of this in Hosea. Israel had gone away from God and was referred to as the Lord's adulterous wife. God is speaking to Israel when He says, "When Israel was a youth I loved him, and out of Egypt I called My son" (Hosea 11:1). The original hearers could conclude, and rightly so, that this referred to Israel's deliverance from Egypt under Moses. But Matthew quotes this passage and says it is prophetic of Jesus Christ when Mary and Joseph returned with Him to Nazareth. "He was there [in Egypt] until the death of Herod, that what was spoken by the Lord through the prophet might be fulfilled, saying, 'Out of Egypt did I call My Son'" (Matthew 2:15).

We note that the Hosea passage is prophetic because Matthew, writing by inspiration of the Holy Spirit, says it is. In your Bible study you may not take such liberties.

Matthew could because he wrote by inspiration of the Spirit, and the Spirit knew the correct interpretation of Hosea since He inspired that also. Matthew, however, does not tell you why he uses the prophecy from Hosea in that way.

Often a prophecy is partially fulfilled in one generation with the remainder fulfilled at another time. At the time when the prophecy is given this is not apparent. It becomes clear when a part is fulfilled and the other is not. It would be much like your looking toward the mountains and seeing but one range. As the prophets looked toward the coming Messiah they saw His two advents as one. As you climb the mountain and descend into the valley on the other side, you see a second range of mountains. You look behind you and see a range; you look in front of you and see another. Christians today are like this in that they stand between the two advents of Christ. Behind us was His first coming; in front of us is His second coming.

We can see in a couple of prophecies that this is what happened. God prophesied through Joel, "It will come about after this that I will pour out My Spirit on all mankind; and your sons and daughters will prophesy, your old men will dream dreams, your young men will see visions. And even on the male and female servants I will pour out My Spirit in those days. And I will display wonders in the sky and on the earth, blood, fire, and columns of smoke. The sun will be turned into darkness, and the moon into blood, before the great and awesome day of the Lord comes. And it will come about that whoever calls on the name of the Lord will be delivered; for on Mount Zion and in Jerusalem there will be those who escape, as the Lord has said, even among the survivors whom the Lord calls" (Joel 2:28-32).

Peter quotes these exact words on the Day of Pentecost (Acts 2:15-21). When the Spirit descended on the church Peter said, "This is what was spoken of through the Prophet

Joel" (Acts 2:16). Indeed the Spirit was poured out upon them. But when did the sun turn into darkness and the moon into blood, "before the great and awesome day of the Lord comes"? This portion of Joel's prophecy refers to the Second Advent and will be fulfilled in the future. From Joel's perspective the two advents appeared as one.

We can observe the same thing in Isaiah's prophecy concerning the Messiah. "The Spirit of the Lord God is upon Me, because the Lord has anointed Me to bring Good News to the afflicted; He has sent Me to bind up the brokenhearted, to proclaim liberty to captives, and freedom to prisoners; to proclaim the favorable year of the Lord, and the day of vengeance of our God; to comfort all who mourn" (Isaiah 61:1, 2).

Jesus was in His hometown of Nazareth when He went into the synagogue to worship on the Sabbath. "The Book of the Prophet Isaiah was handed to Him. And He opened the book, and found the place where it was written, 'The Spirit of the Lord is upon Me, because He anointed Me to preach the Gospel to the poor. He has sent Me to proclaim release to the captives, and recovery of sight to the blind, to set free those who are downtrodden, to proclaim the favorable year of the Lord.' And He closed the book, and gave it back to the attendant, and sat down; and the eyes of all in the synagogue were fixed upon Him. And He began to say to them, 'Today this Scripture has been fulfilled in your hearing' " (Luke 4:17-21).

As you compare the Nazareth declaration with the prophecy in Isaiah, you note that Jesus stopped reading in the middle of the sentence (Isaiah 61:2). He left out the words, "and the day of vengeance of our God; to comfort all that mourn." This part of the prophecy refers to Christ's second coming. Isaiah combined the prophecy regarding the two advents. From his vantage point they appeared as one.

Recognizing this will help you in your Bible study as well as encourage your heart. For the fulfillment of the first installment is a guarantee of its total fulfillment; just as the Holy Spirit is a down payment or guarantee of your inheritance in Christ. Be encouraged. He came the first time as promised. He will come the second time also, as prophesied!

4 Historical Principles of Interpretation

The historical principles deal with the historical setting of the text. To whom and by whom was the book written? Why was it written and what role did the historical setting play in shaping the message of the book? What are the customs and surroundings of the people? These are the kinds of questions you try to answer when considering the historical aspect of your study.

* * *

RULE EIGHTEEN

Since Scripture originated in a historical context, it can be understood only in the light of biblical history.

As you begin your study of a passage, imagine yourself to be a reporter searching for all the facts. Bombard the text with

questions such as:
- To whom was the letter (book) written?
- What was the background of the writer?
- What was the experience or occasion that gave rise to the message?
- Who are the main characters in the book?

Your objective is to place yourself into the setting at the time the book was written and feel with the people involved. What were their concerns? How did God view their situation? Feel the pulse, if you can, of the author as he expresses himself.

A brief background on the Book of Galatians may help bring the importance of this rule into focus.

The New Testament church as God gave it birth was Jewish. The chosen people of the Old Testament were Hebrews and it was from among the Jews that Jesus chose His disciples. On the Day of Pentecost (Acts 2) the non-Jews or Gentiles who were converted were all proselytes of or converts to Judaism. These early followers of Jesus *assumed* that the way to Christ was through the Jewish religion. This was *not* so much a matter of conviction; it was simply the way it happened.

Then Cornelius came to Christ without being circumcised into Judaism (Acts 10), and this caused no small stir among the believers. But this soon quieted down and the subject did not present itself again till the ministry of Paul got under way. Paul, the great scholar of Judaism who was tutored by the famous Rabbi Gamaliel, was God's chosen instrument to refine the doctrine of how Gentiles could become Christians.

While on his first missionary journey, Paul began including Gentile converts in the fellowship of the church without first bringing them through the laws of Judaism. To many Jewish Christians this was unacceptable. The more legalistic of them began to follow Paul's ministry through the Roman province of Galatia (modern-day Turkey), preaching that these Gentile Christians had to be circumcised into the Jewish religion.

Paul was furious. But what could he do? The only Scriptures the church had at that time were the books of the Old Testament, and the Old Testament was what these Judaizers were preaching to the Galatians. When he returned to Jerusalem, Paul attended a council of the church leaders and posed the question to them (Acts 15). Does a Gentile need to become a Jew first before becoming a Christian? How is a man justified before God? "By faith apart from the works of the law" was Paul's contention.

The leadership at the Jerusalem council agreed with Paul. This marked a major change in the direction of the church. Before this Christianity was not considered to be a separate religion. It was viewed as the natural evolution of Judaism—its fulfillment. From this point on Christianity began to be seen as distinct from the Jewish religion.

How was Paul going to share this news with the Galatians? How could he undo the damage caused by the Judaizers? By building his argument on the same basis as the Judaizers. Paul turned to Old Testament law and proved from the law that the law cannot save. Throughout the letter to the Galatians numerous quotes come from the Old Testament law. The Old Testament law, not Paul, preaches that a man is justified by faith apart from the law.

Understanding the historical background helps in understanding and interpreting the Book of Galatians. This type of study will pay rich dividends and you will find it indispensable in the interpretation of any passage you study.

RULE NINETEEN

Though God's revelation in the Scriptures is progressive, both Old and New Testaments are essential parts of this revelation and form a unit.

It is not uncommon to hear a person say, "The God of the Old Testament is different from the God of the New Testament. In the Old Testament He seems so harsh and judgmental, while in the New Testament He is more loving and gracious." Though this is a commonly held belief, it is not based on fact and, if held, will lead you astray in your interpretation of the Bible. For example, Jesus talked more about hell and the judgment of God than did anyone else in the Bible.

The Old Testament sets the stage for the correct interpretation of the New Testament. You would have difficulty understanding what the New Testament is talking about if you were unfamiliar with the Old Testament account of such events as the creation and the fall of man. Jesus assumes that His listeners are familiar with the account of how the Israelites were bitten by serpents for their murmurings and delivered by looking to a serpent of brass placed on a pole (Numbers 21). Referring to this event Jesus said, "As Moses lifted up the serpent in the wilderness, even so must the Son of Man be lifted up" (John 3:14).

In another sense, the New Testament is a commentary on the Old Testament—how God revealed Himself and how His plan is progressive. The further you read, the more you know about Him and what He plans to do. The New Testament explains the purpose of much that happened in the Old Testament.

The whole Book of Hebrews is an example of this. Unless you are familiar with the Old Testament tabernacle, priesthood and sacrificial systems, you will have difficulty following the argument in the book. This letter explains the purpose and significance of the Old Testament forms of worship.

People were saved in Old Testament times the same way they are saved in the New. Justification before God has always been by faith. In the Old Testament people were saved by faith in Christ (the Messiah) who *was* to come. In the New Testament we are saved by faith in Christ who *has* come. Jesus said, "I am the way, and the truth, and the life; no one comes to the Father, but through Me" (John 14:6). This is as true for the Old Testament as for the New Testament.

The means and content of this salvation become progressively clearer as Old Testament history unfolds. The Prophet Isaiah understood more than Adam, but not as much as we do today. But it is clear that there is a unity between the Old and New Testaments on how people are saved.

The unity of the Scriptures can also be seen in the frequent quotations of the Old Testament in the New. Matthew, showing that Jesus is the fulfillment of the Old Testament prophecies, quotes about 70 times from the Old Testament.

From the fall of Adam to the consummation of history all people need Christ as their Redeemer. All believers are born anew by the Holy Spirit. All receive the same inheritance of heaven. God used different methods to communicate these truths. For example, in the Old Testament one of the signs and seals of the covenant relationship was the observance of the Passover and the eating of the paschal lamb; in the New Testament it is the celebration of the Lord's Supper. But the truths themselves are applicable in both testaments.

God does progressively reveal Himself as history unfolds. But this does not mean that God's standards become progressively higher or that God changes along the way.

Rather, it is our understanding of God and His revelation that is progressive. God never changes.

Certain practices in the Old Testament were cancelled by the New Testament, but that is only because they found their fulfillment in Christ. An example of this is the offering of animal sacrifices. When Christ, the perfect sacrifice, offered Himself, there was no longer a need to offer animals. These animal sacrifices were a preview of what God planned to do through Jesus Christ. But the Scriptures make it quite clear that animal sacrifices could not save, "for it is impossible for the blood of bulls and goats to take away sins" (Hebrews 10:4).

God's character in the Old Testament did not change by some process of moral evolution. His perfect holiness is an unchanging, uncompromising part of His nature. For example, Jesus was interrogated on the subject of divorce (Matthew 19). Some argued in its favor on the basis of the law of divorce in the Mosaic code. "Why then," they asked, "did Moses command to give her a certificate and divorce her?" (verse 7; see Deuteronomy 24:1-4)

Jesus replied, "Because of your hardness of heart, Moses permitted you to divorce your wives; but from the beginning it has not been this way" (verse 8). Jesus said that the laws against divorce were temporarily set aside in the Old Testament because of the moral callousness of the people, not because of any change in the character of God or His moral requirements.

God's revelation of Himself is progressive as you read through the Bible, but His character is unchanging. God's great plan of redemption is the same in both testaments. As you study the Bible you can consider them two parts of the same book, not two separate books.

RULE TWENTY

Historical facts or events become symbols of spiritual truths only if the Scriptures so designate them.

Webster defines *symbol* as "something that stands for or suggests something else by reason or relationship, association, convention, or accidental resemblance; especially a visible sign of something invisible." Though there are differences between the words *symbol*, *type*, *allegory*, *simile* and *metaphor*, they are closely enough related to combine them here. This rule applies to all of them since they are often used as visible signs of something invisible.

An example of the Bible's use of a historical event as a symbol of a spiritual truth is Paul's statement: "I do not want you to be unaware, brethren, that our fathers were all under the cloud, and all passed through the sea; and all were baptized into Moses in the cloud and in the sea; and all ate the same spiritual food; and all drank the same spiritual drink, for they were drinking from a spiritual rock which followed them; and the rock was Christ" (I Corinthians 10:1-4).

Israel's passing through the Red Sea (Exodus 14:22) symbolized their baptism. The rock from which Israel drank (Numbers 20:11) was a type of Christ. In a number of places the writer borrows from a historical event to represent a spiritual truth.

To carry this further than Paul does would be to detract from the literal meaning of the passage. To say that the Red Sea symbolizes the atoning blood of Christ, which offers a safe way to the heavenly Canaan, is an improper interpretation of the Corinthian passage.

This same rule is also applied to allegorizing. As Paul develops his theme in the Book of Galatians, that justification is through faith in Jesus Christ apart from the law, he uses an allegory to drive home his point. Not only does he allegorize Sarah and Hagar (who both bore Abraham children), he tells us he is doing so. "It is written that Abraham had two sons, one by the bondwoman and one by the free woman. But the son by the bondwoman was born according to the flesh, and the son by the free woman through the promise. This contains an allegory: for these women are two covenants, one proceeding from Mount Sinai bearing children who are to be slaves; she is Hagar" (Galatians 4:22-24).

Paul made these interpretations of the Old Testament under the inspiration of the Holy Spirit. He did so occasionally and for specific reasons. But for you to make a habit of allegorizing historical facts is to detract from the literal interpretation of the Bible and to change its intended meaning. The objective of Bible study is to understand the intended meaning of the author, not to pour into his words your own content.

A negative example often helps, especially when a passage has been used to symbolize something that it should not have.

A common Scripture so used is the Book of Philemon. Paul is writing to his good friend Philemon on behalf of a runaway slave, Onesimus. Onesimus, the slave of Philemon, had robbed his master and fled to Rome. There, through Paul, he became a Christian and Paul was sending him back to his master in Colosse with this letter. Paul's plea to his friend is that he forgive Onesimus and restore him as "a beloved brother." "If he has wronged you in any way, or owes you anything, charge that to my account," was Paul's request (verse 18). It is a beautiful example of Christian love, forgiveness and brotherhood.

For no apparent reason many allegorize this book,

equating Philemon with God, Onesimus with mankind and Paul with Christ. Christ (Paul) intercedes with the Father (Philemon) on behalf of the converted runaway (Onesimus). Paul does not make this analogy here or in any other passage. Neither should you.

This kind of allegorizing is different from making application. For example, we can say that what Paul was asking of Philemon on behalf of Onesimus is what Christ did for us. We should in the same way forgive those who have wronged us. Our application is drawn from the historical event or fact without changing the intended meaning of the fact.

5 Theological Principles of Interpretation

Theology is the study of God and His relation to the world. The source book for this study is the Bible. Theology seeks to draw conclusions on various broad and important topics in the Bible. What is God like? What is the nature of man? What is a proper doctrine of salvation? These are the kinds of subjects with which theology deals. Theological principles are those broad rules that deal with the formation of doctrine. For example, how can we tell if a doctrine is truly biblical? One of our theological principles will seek to answer this.

* * *

RULE TWENTY-ONE
You must understand the Bible grammatically before you can understand it theologically.

Another way to state this rule is to say, "You must understand what the passage says before you can expect to understand what it means." An example of this may be seen in this Pauline statement:

"But the free gift is not like the transgression. For if by the transgression of the one the many died, much more did the grace of God and the gift by the grace of the one Man, Jesus Christ, abound to the many. And the gift is not like that which came through the one who sinned; for on the one hand the judgment arose from one transgression resulting in condemnation, but on the other hand the free gift arose from many transgressions resulting in justification. For if by the transgression of the one, death reigned through the one, much more those who receive the abundance of grace and of the gift of righteousness will reign in life through the One, Jesus Christ.

"So then as through one transgression there resulted condemnation to all men, even so through one act of righteousness there resulted justification of life to all men. For as through the one man's disobedience the many were made sinners, even so through the obedience of the One the many will be made righteous.

"And the law came in that the transgression might increase; but where sin increased, grace abounded all the more, that, as sin reigned in death, even so grace might reign through righteousness to eternal life through Jesus Christ our Lord" (Romans 5:15-21).

You must study this passage carefully to understand what Paul is saying. He is comparing Christ with Adam. Just as you are considered to be unrighteous because of the sin of Adam, so you are considered to be righteous because of what Jesus Christ did. The sin of Adam was imputed to you, even though you did nothing to deserve it; so also the righteousness of Christ was imputed to you, even though you did nothing to deserve it. This, in part, is what the passage says.

From this we can draw certain conclusions. For example, we see that imputation does not affect your moral character, but your legal standing. When you were considered righteous because of the work of Christ your moral character was not changed; you did not become morally righteous and perfect, only legally righteous and perfect in the sight of God. This is why some non-Christians are more righteous in their behavior than Christians.

Another example is this statement: "If we go on sinning willfully after receiving the knowledge of the truth, there no longer remains a sacrifice for sins" (Hebrews 10:26). Many use this verse to teach that it is possible for a Christian to lose his salvation. A study of this verse in its context leads you to an entirely different conclusion. This passage speaks specifically to Jews who believed in animal sacrifices in anticipation of the coming Messiah, not realizing that He had already come.

The writer to the Hebrews sets forth the fact of Jesus' sacrifice. This statement says that once these Jews understood the reason for Jesus' death and willfully ignored it, if they returned to their sacrifices there would be no future sacrifice provided by God.

You can see how such a problem can be alleviated by using sound grammatical principles (Rules 10-17). You must understand what a passage says before you draw any doctrinal conclusions from it.

RULE TWENTY-TWO

A doctrine cannot be considered biblical unless it sums up and includes all that the Scriptures say about it.

It is immediately apparent that this is an important procedure in Bible study, just as it is in all of life. Solomon warned, "He who gives an answer before he hears, it is folly and shame to him" (Proverbs 18:13). It is foolish to come to a conclusion before hearing all of the arguments. So also, it is a mistake to come to conclusions regarding a certain doctrine before studying all the Bible says on the subject.

For example, there are numerous passages in the New Testament which tell you that you are not under the law. "For we maintain that a man is justified by faith apart from works of the law" (Romans 3:28). "But if you are led by the Spirit, you are not under the law" (Galatians 5:18). When reading such statements, can you conclude that the grace of God frees you from any obligation to live a disciplined, holy life?

Not at all. Such a conclusion would be countered by statements such as: "What shall we say then? Are we to continue in sin that grace might increase? May it never be! How shall we who died to sin still live in it? Or do you not know that all of us who have been baptized into Christ Jesus have been baptized into His death? Therefore we have been buried with Him through baptism into death, in order that as Christ was raised from the dead through the glory of the Father, so we too might walk in newness of life" (Romans 6:1-4).

This is where a topical type of Bible study proves useful. You take a theme, idea or teaching and study all the passages on the subject. Three kinds of parallel studies are:

1. *Word Parallels.* You may, for example, decide to study

the life of Balaam. The main passage regarding him is found in Numbers 22—24. He was one of God's prophets who allowed himself to be enticed by an invitation from the king of Moab to curse Israel. What conclusions can you draw from his life? A study of what the New Testament writers say of Balaam will help in your evaluation. Peter tells us that he "loved the wages of unrighteousness" (II Peter 2:15). Jude tells us that he was greedy for reward (Jude 11). John further informs us that he counseled the king of Moab to "put a stumbling block before the sons of Israel, to eat things sacrificed to idols, and to commit acts of immorality" (Revelation 2:14).

2. *Idea Parallels.* An idea parallel differs from a word parallel in that you can't cross-reference the word, as you can with Balaam. The idea is more encompassing than any one word. An example might be the whole question of authority. The chief priests and elders asked Jesus, "By what authority are You doing these things, and who gave You this authority?" (Matthew 21:23) You would want to study not only this passage in Matthew 21, but many other passages in the Scriptures on the subject. Moses records man's first rebellion against authority (Genesis 3); Scripture also shows God dealing severely with those who rejected the authority of one of His servants (Numbers 16).

3. *Doctrinal Parallels.* This would include topical studies on the great doctrines of the Bible such as the attributes of God, the nature of man, redemption, justification and sanctification.

In this type of study you gather all the pieces of information together and draw a conclusion. It is much like putting the pieces of a puzzle together. This is called *inductive reasoning,* that process of reasoning from all the parts to the whole. If you were going to study the doctrine of the church inductively, for instance, you would find all the passages on the subject, study each one and then put them all together to form your conclusions.

In Rule 24 we will consider a principle dealing with *deductive reasoning,* but we need to look briefly at deductive reasoning here. This is the method that approaches the study by looking at the whole and coming to conclusions regarding the smaller pieces, again, like a jigsaw puzzle. From the whole puzzle you can conclude certain things about the individual pieces. Deductive reasoning is that process of reasoning from the general to the particular. An example of deductive reasoning is:

- *First Premise*—If we ask according to His will, God hears us (I John 5:14, 15).
- *Second Premise*—Sanctification is according to God's will (I Thessalonians 4:3).
- *Conclusion*—When we pray for our sanctification, God hears us.

The reason we are discussing deductive reasoning here is the need to relate it to your inductive study. As a general rule, the first premise in your *deductive* study can be made only after *inductive* study has brought you to the understanding of what that premise is and means. Other examples of *deductive* study may be seen in Rule 24.

Inductive Bible study is extremely important in developing your convictions. As you study the parts you are able to get an increasingly clearer picture of the whole. If you are not involved in an inductive study, you should be. For if your convictions regarding the doctrines of the Bible have been formed by what others have told you, rather than by your own personal investigation of the Scriptures, will they stand during times of testing? You cannot count on remaining faithful during times of adversity on the basis of hearsay. You must dig into the Scriptures for yourself and get your own convictions.

Unfortunately, as is so often the case, what is important requires hard work. This is true in the formation of vital convictions. Careful and thorough Bible study is required. No shortcut exists. Your doctrinal studies form the backbone of your spiritual convictions, and these in turn can be arrived at only by studying all that the Bible says on a given subject.

RULE TWENTY-THREE

When two doctrines taught in the Bible appear to be contradictory, accept both as scriptural in the confident belief that they resolve themselves into a higher unity.

A number of seeming contradictions or paradoxes exist in the Scriptures. "Seeming" because they really are not. They appear contradictory because the finite mind of man cannot comprehend the infinite mind of God.

Some familiar paradoxes to the human mind are:

1. *The Trinity.* We do not serve three Gods, but one, yet *each* Person in the Godhead is fully and completely God, not just one-third God. In essence we must conclude that one plus one plus one equals one. No human illustration can adequately explain this theological mystery. It is utterly beyond our comprehension.

2. *The dual nature of Christ.* Jesus Christ is all God and all Man. He is not half God and half man, yet He is not two persons, but one. Again one plus one equals one.

3. *The origin and existence of evil.* Logically the human mind deduces that one of two things must be true. Either God created evil, or it is coeternal with Him. The Bible leads us to believe that neither is true. It is a mystery.

4. *The sovereign election of God and the responsibility of man.* Paul states that God has chosen the believer in His sovereign counsel before the foundation of the world (Ephesians 1:4). Yet Peter says, "The Lord is not slow about His promise, as some count slowness, but is patient toward you, not wishing for any to perish but for all to come to repentance" (II Peter 3:9). All through the Scriptures there is a well-meant offer of the Gospel to all men. Man is viewed as a responsible moral agent who is held accountable by

God, and "whoever will call upon the name of the Lord will be saved" (Romans 10:13). There is no way that our minds can reconcile these two difficult and seemingly opposite truths.

Of all the difficulties none causes as much emotional controversy as the last one. Possibly this is because the first three strike us as rather academic, while the fourth touches our moral sensibilities. It has to do with man's eternal destiny.

When the Bible leaves two conflicting doctrines unreconciled, so must you. Living in tension is not pleasant, but you must take care not to lose biblical balance in seeking to relieve the tension. Do not wrench the Scriptures apart in an attempt to force two conflicting doctrines into compromise.

You can make application of such conflicting doctrines by preaching the right doctrine to the right person. For example, as a Christian you preach to yourself that God chose you; you did not choose Him. If the choice had been yours, you would have voted *against* Him. All you are and have is a gift of God's grace. This should fill you with humility and meekness.

But you can boldly proclaim to the non-Christian that God loves him. For Jesus Himself said, "God so loved the *world,* that He gave His only begotten Son" (John 3:16).

Our allegiance is not first and primarily to a system of theology, but to the Scripture. When you interpret the Bible, don't allow human logic to make it say any more or less than it in fact says. To the degree that the Scriptures speak with clarity, you may speak with clarity. When the Scriptures are silent, you must remain silent. Where the Bible teaches two "conflicting" doctrines, you must follow its example and hold to both, keeping each in perfect balance with the other

RULE TWENTY-FOUR

A teaching merely implied in Scripture may be considered biblical when a comparison of related passages supports it.

The Jewish religious community in Jesus' time was split into various groups: Herodians, Essenes, Zealots, Sadducees and Pharisees. These last two groups were divided over certain doctrinal issues, notably the resurrection of the dead. The Pharisees believed it; the Sadducees denied it.

On one occasion Jesus found Himself in an argument with the Sadducees on this question of the afterlife. Did the Old Testament really teach it? Listen to Jesus' line of reasoning, "Regarding the fact that the dead rise again, have you not read in the Book of Moses, in the passage about the burning bush, how God spoke to him, saying, 'I am the God of Abraham, and the God of Isaac, and the God of Jacob'? He is not the God of the dead, but of the living; you are greatly mistaken" (Mark 12:26, 27).

The Lord said that the resurrection could be proved from the Old Testament (Exodus 3:15), where God identified Himself as the God of Abraham, Isaac and Jacob. Since God is the God of the living, these three men must be alive or resurrected. This is deductive reasoning, and could be charted in the following form:

- *First Premise*—God is the God of the living.
- *Second Premise*—God is the God of Abraham, Isaac and Jacob.
- *Conclusion*—Abraham, Isaac and Jacob are among the living.

The doctrine of the resurrection is *implied* in the Old Testament, reasoned Christ. It is not expressly stated in the. Old Testament that there is a resurrection of the dead, but when you compare related passages on the subject you deduce that such is true.

Another example is the question of admitting women to the Lord's Table. We conclude that they should be admitted to communion, but not on the basis of any specific command or example in the Bible, since none is given. We assume that they should be admitted on the basis of the *implied* teachings of the New Testament. In this example, the deductive process is as follows:

When Paul wrote to the Corinthian church, it is obvious that women were members of the church. "For I have been informed concerning you, my brethren, by Chloe's people, that there are quarrels among you" (I Corinthians 1:11). "The churches of Asia greet you. Aquila and Prisca greet you heartily in the Lord, with the church that is in their house" (I Corinthians 16:19). Both Chloe and Priscilla were women. Paul also instructed the church on how to conduct itself at the Lord's Supper (I Corinthians 11). Therefore we infer from these passages of Scripture that women partook of communion.

- *First Premise*—The Corinthian church received instruction on communion.
- *Second Premise*—Women were part of the church at Corinth.
- *Conclusion*—Women may partake in communion.

You must be certain the deductions you make are truly implied in the Scriptures from which you derive them, and that you have investigated and compared related passages on the subject. It is easy to misuse the principle and arrive at unbiblical conclusions. This is frequently done with passages that give us examples from the life of Christ.

Mark says of Jesus, "In the early morning, while it was still dark, He arose and went out and departed to a lonely place, and was praying there" (Mark 1:35). From this we are

likely to deduce that a faithful Christian should have his
quiet time in the early morning.

- *First Premise*—The believer is to be Christlike.
- *Second Premise*—Christ had early morning devotions.
- *Conclusion*—The believer should have early morning
  devotions.

Yet, you will remember that under Rule 5, *Biblical
examples are authoritative only when supported by a
command,* we discussed this, using this very example. Using
the reasoning spelled out here you can properly conclude
that you *may* have early morning devotions, but not that you
must have them. This passage supports the validity of the
quiet time in the morning, but not its necessity.

You cannot violate one principle of interpretation in
order to substantiate another. Your Bible study must take all
the principles into account if you are to make a proper
interpretation.

Believing something to be true because of an implied
teaching in the Bible is not only valid, but also necessary
(Jesus' argument for the resurrection from the Old Testament, for example). Like Rule 23, however, such reasoning
requires careful study, and this is hard work; but the fruit of
such labor is rewarding and well worth the effort.

Do not be afraid to use deductive reasoning in your Bible
study. In everyday life, you do it all the time. Suppose you
are working for a data processing firm and you have been on
this job for some time. Today, as you are going to work, you
find yourself returning to that job even though your
employer did not specifically ask you to come in this day.
You are doing it because you reason:

- *First Premise*—Your employer wants you as an
  employee.
- *Second Premise*—Your employer has had you on this
  particular job for some time.

- *Conclusion*—Your employer wants you on that job today.

Think back on the number of times you have *deduced* something to be true on the basis of certain facts; or how someone *implied* something to be true even though he did not specifically say so.

This process is valid in your Bible study as well, providing you abide carefully by Rule 24.

Summary and Conclusion

It has been the aim of this book to provide simple ground rules of interpretation that would lead you to a more accurate and consequently more rewarding Bible study program. Twenty-four rules with half a dozen or so corollaries may seem like a rather large plate of food to digest, but you can do it. Actually much of what we read soon leaves the conscious mind and slips into the subconscious. Only when some related thought or experience triggers what is stored there does it surface to the conscious once again.

As you engage in Bible study, the process of interpreting the Scriptures will trigger the thoughts of this book now stored in your subconscious mind and bring them to the surface. You can refer to the ground rule in question and refresh your memory on its application. Before long, these rules will become almost second nature to you—much like striking the keys of the piano for an accomplished pianist.

To the degree that they are valid, the rules contained in this book should be biblically self-evident. As you read

them, they should have appeared obvious. If you entertain
the possibility of substituting an alternative for any one of
the rules, the implications of such a change should make it
unacceptable.

For example, Rule 12 reads, *Interpret a word in relation
to its sentence and context.* Let's suggest as an alternative
that we *not* interpret a word in light of its context, but solely
on the basis of what the dictionary says. Then Paul is
referring to four-legged animals when he refers to "dogs"
(Philippians 3:2), and King Herod is a literal "fox" (Luke
13:32).

These rules, if they are sound and accurate, conform with
the spirit and content of what the Bible states is true.

There may have been a time, say a generation or so ago,
when writing out such self-evident rules was unnecessary.
But in today's society things have changed; our relativistic
generation questions absolutes and blurs issues; and the
setting down of rules of interpretation for Bible study has
become a necessity. That which is self-evident to a biblically
knowledgeable people strikes those unfamiliar with the
Bible as new.

This has its good and bad sides. It is a fact that the
Scriptures are fresh and alive for the man on the street today.
Again and again hungry young men and women are drawn
out of relativistic thinking and into an encounter with the
dynamic truths of the Bible. That which was embedded in
the minds of our forefathers as being "obvious" to the point
of being dry is today viewed as new and startling—and that
is appealing to people.

The disadvantage is that we have produced a generation
of biblical illiterates who not only are unfamiliar with the
great truths of the Scriptures, but are unsure of how to go
about discovering them. So a basic and simple approach to
the principles of biblical interpretation is a great need today.

In seeking to apply these rules you must remember that there is a difference between the rules being biblically correct, and using them properly. A hammer is the correct tool to drive in a nail, but using a hammer does not guarantee that you won't bend the nail. As you apply these rules of interpretation to your Bible study you are not guaranteed a correct interpretation at every try. You will make mistakes. But hopefully proficiency and accuracy will come with faithful practice.

There may have been times as you read through these chapters that you felt you were "left hanging" as to what the proper interpretation of a passage should be. Though it was not the intent to leave the reader "hanging," the book did try to keep from interpreting the passages for you.

The goal of the book has been the establishment of ground rules for interpretation, not interpretation itself. Unfortunately this has not always been possible. Traces of the author's theological bias crept in, though hopefully at a minimum.

Some have suggested a lab session on some of the passages. An exposition of I John 3:6-10 on pages 65-66 afforded such an opportunity. Another suggestion was to expound a passage using as many of the ground rules as possible.

These suggestions were appealing, but would no doubt have detracted from the purpose of the book. We would forever be debating whether the right conclusion was drawn from a particular rule. Therefore the meaning of each of the 24 rules was explained, and their application left to you.

If you feel that you are just a beginner in the art of properly interpreting the Bible, be encouraged to take bold steps forward. Don't fasten your eyes on the possible mistakes you may make, but on the incomparable Christ and the rich potential you have of getting to know Him better.

1. Work from the assumption the Bible is authoritat[ive]
2. The Bible interprets itself - Scripture best explains Scr[ipture]
3. Saving faith & the H.S. are necessary to understand &
   properly interpret Scriptures
4. Interpret personal experiences in light of Scripture &
   not Scripture in light of personal exper[ience]
5. Biblical examples are authoritative only when
   supported by a command.
6. The primary purpose of the Bible is to chg our live[s]
   not increase our knowledge
7. Each Christian has the rt & responsibility to investi[gate]
   & interpret the Word of God for himself.
8. Church hist. is impo but not decisive in the
   interpretation of Scripture.
9. The promises of God throuout the Bible are availabl[e]
   to the H.S. for the believers of every generation
10. Scripture has only 1 meaning & should be tak[en]
    literally.

11.